Perfume
Bottles

A Collector's Guide

Perfume Bottles

Bottles

A Collector's Guide

Madeleine Marsh

Special Consultants:
Linda Bee and Lynda Brine

MILLER'S PERFUME BOTTLES: A COLLECTOR'S GUIDE
by Madeleine Marsh
Special consultants: Linda Bee and Lynda Brine

First published in Great Britain in 1999 by Miller's, a division of
Mitchell Beazley, imprints of Octopus Publishing Group Ltd,
Michelin House, 81 Fulham Road, London SW3 6RB

First published in USA in 1999
Copyright © Octopus Publishing Group Ltd
Miller's is a registered trademark of Octopus Publishing Group Ltd
This edition distributed in the USA by Antique Collectors' Club Ltd.
Market Street Industrial Park, Wappinger's Falls, NY 12590, USA

Executive Editor **Alison Starling**
Executive Art Editor **Vivienne Brar**
Editor **Elisabeth Faber**
Designer **Lou Griffiths & Adrian Morris**
Indexer **Sue Farr**
Picture Research **Jenny Faithfull**
Production **Rachel Staveley**

Specially commissioned photography by **Tim Ridley**
Jacket photograph: **Stuart Chorley**
Jacket illustration, left to right: "Hattie Carnegie", 1938; Victorian cut-glass
silver-topped perfume bottle; Czech glass perfume bottle, 1930s; "Prince
Matchabelli", 1930s–1950s; Chanel "No.19", 1950s

The publishers will be grateful for any information that will assist them in
keeping future editions up to date. Although all reasonable care has been
taken in the preparation of this book, neither the publishers nor the compilers
can accept any liability for any consequence arising from the use thereof,
or the information contained therein.

ISBN 1 84000 162 3

A CIP catalogue record for this book is available from the British Library

Set in Bembo, Frutiger and Shannon
Colour reproduction by Vimnice Printing Press Co. Ltd., Hong Kong
Produced by Toppan Printing Co., (HK) Ltd.
Printed and bound in China

contents

Introduction

Nothing stirs the memory like perfume. You never forget the scent your mother wore or the fragrance used by a lover. A single sniff can transport the mind over years and miles. Russian astronauts went into space with flasks of essential oils to remind them of Earth, and from the time of its earliest use perfume was believed to put man in touch with the heavens.

The word perfume comes from the Latin per fumum ("through smoke"). Antique civilizations burnt aromatic substances in their temples to please the gods and to counteract the smell of burning flesh during sacrifice – thousands of years later, incense is still part of religious ritual. Across the ancient world perfume was crucial to the death ceremony. The dead were buried with flasks of aromatic oils, and in Egypt corpses were embalmed with myrrh and cassia, and wrapped in scented bandages both as a symbol of eternity and to preserve the body from putrefaction. Perfume filtered into secular use. Cosmetic oils were used after the bath, and served at Greek and Roman banquets. Classical authors tell of scented doves flying fragrantly around the room, and of statues sprinkling wine and perfume from every orifice. Emperor Nero was hugely extravagant in his use of perfume; on one infamous occasion he spent the equivalent of £100,000 on a waterfall of rose petals that smothered and killed one of his guests.

With the collapse of the Roman Empire, perfume for pleasure was discouraged, and it was not until the Crusaders returned with new spices and ointments from the East that the art of perfumery flourished again in Western courts. When Catherine de' Medici married the French King Henry II in 1533, she brought her own personal perfumer from Italy, and established a perfume laboratory at Grasse in Provence. In England, Elizabeth I was famous for her love of perfume. The rooms of her palace were sprinkled with scent from silver casting bottles, her clothes were hung with sweet bags, her leather gloves and even her shoes were steeped in favourite blends of musk and damask roses. In one year alone she spent £40 with her "stillers of sweet waters". As a courtier noted: "The sharpness of her nose was equalled only by the sharpness of her tongue."

In the 16thC and 17thC, perfume was used to conceal a lack of hygiene, and was not only valued for its cosmetic purposes. Scented pomanders, worn as necklaces or carried in the hand, were believed to ward off plague and other infections, and many curative powers were attributed to perfume.

Pleasure, however, became the most important principle. The 18thC saw both the establishment of a number of major perfume houses (Yardley and Houbigant were both founded in 1775) and the creation of handsome and costly flasks for a wealthy clientele. Whereas the beaux and beauties of the Regency were extravagant in their use of strong-smelling perfumes, Victorian ladies favoured gentle floral waters, sprinkled on handkerchiefs and clothing rather than applied directly to the skin. Vast numbers of scent bottles were produced in the 19thC, and with improved industrial techniques and the development of synthetic fragrances, flacons and containers were no longer just the preserve of the rich, but were targeted at a far wider audience. This heralded a dramatic change in manufacture.

For centuries, ladies had either made their own scent or had it blended by the perfumer and decanted into their personal bottles. The turn of the century saw the emergence of the commercial perfume industry as we know it today, with women buying ready-made named brands over the counter – fragrance, bottle, and box sold together as a complete presentation, the glamour of the perfume inseparable from its specially designed packaging.

In the 20thC, pioneering commercial perfumers such as Coty and Guerlain found themselves competing with new rivals as well as each other. In 1921, Coco Chanel was the first couturier to lend her name to a perfume, recognizing that Chanel "No.5" could be an affordable luxury for those who could not aspire to buy her clothes, and launching a trend that has been the economic mainstay of the fashion industry ever since. The first half of the 20thC was a golden age for presentations. Bottles reflected every artistic style, from Art Nouveau to Surrealism, and conjured up the glamour of the great couture houses. New materials such as Bakelite and other forms of plastic led to cheaper packaging, and the market expanded. With the rise of mass production after World War II, cheap, fun fragrances were targeted at a new teenage audience.

Perfume is still one of our favourite luxuries. The fragrance industry is worth between $660 and $825 million a year in Britain alone, and more than 50 percent of the female population receive perfume as a gift. Fortunes are spent on developing and marketing new fragrances, and flacons are still created by top designers.

The charm of perfume is fugitive, but the bottles it came in have lasted for hundreds and thousands of years, an enduring symbol of one of man's greatest, invisible pleasures.

Prices & dimensions

Prices for antiques vary, depending on the condition of the item, geographical location, and market trends, so the price ranges given throughout this book should be seen as guides to value only.

Abbreviations used for dimensions are as follows: ht height; l. length; w. width; diam. diameter. Dimensions are given in centimetres and inches.
Conversion rate: $1.65 = £1.00

Collecting advice

Perfume bottle collecting has grown hugely in popularity over the past decade, and there is an overwhelming choice of items to collect, ranging from the bottles themselves to a host of related ephemera. Collectors' clubs have sprung up around the world; there are specialist dealers and auctions, and even contemporary perfumers now bring out limited-edition bottles aimed at the collectors' market.

What to collect

The earliest scent flasks known to man date from antiquity, and, across the millennia, bottles have been produced in an infinite variety of designs and materials. There are enthusiasts for everything from Egyptian ointment jars to Avon bottles, from Victorian glass to modern miniatures. Some might concentrate on the works of an individual glassmaker (Lalique, Baccarat), or the products of a particular perfumer or fashion house (Guerlain, Schiaparelli). Others will collect bottles by shape (animals, figures), by medium (silver, porcelain), or by period. The possibilities are endless, but basically collectors tend to focus on two main areas: non-commercial and commercial bottles. The first category – the standard bottles available until the end of the 19thC – includes scent containers made for a lady's or gentleman's personal use, into which he or she would decant the perfume that either had been bought from a perfumer or mixed personally. The second category, mainly 20thC, covers commercial perfume presentations (bottle, box, and packaging) designed for a named perfume, and conceived and sold by the manufacturer as a complete product.

This book covers both non-commercial and commercial scent bottles. Objects illustrated date from antiquity to the present day, and every item is given a detailed description and a contemporary price range. This reflects what one would expect to pay for an item, not its selling price to a dealer. It is also important to remember that estimates in saleroom catalogues do not take into account the commission that the buyer will have to pay on top of the hammer price. Values will fluctuate, depending on many different factors, and the price ranges here should only be used as a guideline.

Collecting tips

• It is not just famous name perfumes that are collectible. With Chanel "No.5", for example, the shape of the flacon has changed so little since its launch that even the earliest pieces fetch comparatively low prices. However, unsuccessful perfumes or bottle designs, produced for a limited period of time, have the appeal of rarity that attracts enthusiasts.

• With commercial perfumes, the same bottle design could have been produced by a number of different glassworks over the years. Examples by the more prestigious makers (e.g. Lalique, Baccarat) tend to be the most desirable.

• To assist dating, look inside the lid of commercial screw-top bottles. Pre-1960s tops often have foil, cork or rubber linings, while post-1960s interiors tend to be plastic.

• Fragranced perfume cards (see p.57) are becoming increasingly collectible and can be safely stored in photograph albums.

• Boxes can have a value in their own right, and collectors will buy empty packaging in the hopes of one day reuniting a box with its original bottle.

Condition

- Examine the bottle for damage and chips. Vulnerable areas include the base, neck, and stopper, and parts with raised decoration.
- When buying silver-topped flasks, check hinges for breakage, and see that screw-on lids still fit securely.
- Ensure that glass stoppers are original and fit the neck of the bottle. On some flacons, the base of both bottle and stopper will have been marked with the same number, thus proving that they belong together.
- Always check the base and body of a bottle for any mark, signature, or label.
- Silver hallmarks can help identify the exact date and nationality of a flacon (see p.17).
- With atomizers, check that rubber bulbs have not perished, and that silk coverings are still intact.
- Bottles in their original packaging command a premium. What the collector of commercial presentations really wants is the whole marketing package: bottle and box, complete with any extra tags, labels, or other ephemera. Do not throw away packaging, no matter how worn or damaged it is, as even this can enhance a bottle's value. However, packaging in good condition is always more desirable.
- Bottles are worth more if they are unopened and still filled with their original fragrance, also known as the "juice".

Care & cleaning

- Take great care with cleaning. Wash bottles in a plastic bowl or over a rubber mat and dry with a soft cloth. Interiors can be dried with a hair dryer. Only non-commercial bottles, with no labels or perfume left inside them, should be cleaned this way. Commercial bottles should be spot-cleaned only, or simply left alone.
- Gilding, enameling, and hand-tinted surfaces can all be damaged by over-enthusiastic rubbing. Do not scrub and avoid abrasive cleaners.
- On commercial bottles, labels can be ruined or taken off by water or cleaning agents, so dust or spot clean rather than wash.
- Glass stoppers that are stuck can be removed by holding the bottle under warm running water or stroking vegetable oil around the neck. Twist stoppers with care.
- The interiors of bottles can be cleaned with soap and water and a small bottle-brush. More stubborn stains can be removed with alcohol or nail-polish remover, although the residue should then be rinsed out. Use a small funnel or a pipette.
- If a bottle has contained smelling salts or aromatic vinegars, the interior of the glass can become clouded; it will be impossible to restore it to its original state.
- With commercial bottles, the original perfume can enhance the value of the flask, and if a bottle is sealed it should not be opened.
- Keep bottles out of direct sunlight. This can cause labels to fade, and contents to evaporate, and can also affect the bottle's surface. Avoid keeping bottles in extreme temperatures, as this can cause them to crack or even shatter.
- When transporting bottles, fold each one in tissue paper or plastic bubble wrap, and wrap glass stoppers individually.

Ancient bottles

The earliest perfume bottles known date from antiquity, and most of the flacons illustrated here were excavated from tombs. Across the ancient world, the dead were buried with flasks of perfumed oils to ease their journey to the afterlife. When Howard Carter opened up Tutankhamun's tomb in 1922, alabaster unguent jars surrounding the young king still smelled faintly of spikenard (an aromatic herb) after 3,000 years. In many cultures perfume was crucial to religious ceremonies; scented oils were used for libations, incense was burnt to appease the gods, and in Arabia, celebrated for its production of spices and resins, musk was even mixed into the mortar of temple buildings so that they would smell sweet in the heat of the sun. Perfume was also essential to secular life, employed for health, as part of the bathing process, and above all for cosmetic pleasure.

Left to right: alabaster perfume vial, 1st millennium BC, **$132–165**; pottery ointment jar, glazed turquoise blue and painted with hieroglyphics, **$1,237–1,320**

▼ Egyptian containers

The Egyptians were famous for their use of rich perfumes and cosmetics. Small flasks such as these would have held scented oils and makeup: kohl to line the eyes, henna to stain the lips, and green eye paint, from powdered malachite. These oils and pastes were both decorative and protective, guarding the skin against the rays of the sun. The small perfume vial (far left) is alabaster, a popular material since it was soft enough to drill, non-porous, and kept the scent cool. The blue-glazed ointment jar (left) is decorated with hieroglyphics showing the name of the son of Pharaoh Rameses II.

◄ Core glass

Found in Syria, this amphora was made by the core technique, which preceded blowing, introduced by the Syrians c.100BC. An inner core of mud and straw was coated with molten glass. The surface was then decorated with trails of colored glass and combed with a toothed metal tool to make a festooned pattern. Once the glass had cooled, the inner core was scraped out. Even after some 2,500 years, this oil bottle is in fine condition, its design and decoration still beautiful and remarkably well preserved.

Phoenician amphora, found in Syria, 4th–3rdC BC, **$4,290–4,620**

▼Double flask

This glass double flask (or unguentarium) has an inverted heart-shaped handle, and could be held in the hand, or hung from a wall or a belt. The vials are still filled with earth from the site where this bottle was dug up. Great care should be taken when cleaning such pieces. The iridescent colors that distinguish early glass were not just integral to the metal but are also the result of being buried, and of the oxidizing process of metallic salts in sand and soil. This surface patina is crucial to the charm and value of such antique remains.

▼Blown glass

After its discovery in Syria, the technique of blowing glass spread rapidly throughout the Roman Empire. The mold-blown flask below, green in tone with a flaring rim and a folded edge, is a typical shape, and would probably have been used for storing rose water. The Romans loved this fragrance, and, according to legend, Emperor Nero had silver pipes installed in his palace so that visitors were sprinkled with rose water.

Roman blown glass bottle, 1st–3rdC AD, **$660–742**

Double unguentarium, 1st–3rdC AD, **$1,072–1,555**

Left to right: Roman tear bottle, used for cosmetics and perfume, 1st–4thC AD, **$58–82**; small glass container (ht 5cm/1 ¼in), Persian, 700–800 AD, **$58–66**

Men and perfume

In the ancient world, men used perfume as much as, if not more than, women. Bath houses were often for men only, and after sweating and plunging it was customary to rub down with scented oils, as recorded by the Athenian playwright Antiphanes, writing in the 4thC BC: "He steeps his feet and legs in rich Egyptian unguents; his jaws and breasts he rubs with thick palm oil, and both his arms with extract of sweet mint; his eyebrows and his hair with marjoram; his knees and neck with essence of ground thyme."

▼Tear bottles

Long-necked bottles, such as the Roman flask (below left), are often found in tombs. Early scholars dubbed them lacrymatories or tear bottles, assuming that they were used to hold the tears of the bereaved. Chemical tests, however, have disproved this romantic theory, revealing traces of oil and essences. Small antiquities such as these survive in some number; the collecting base is small, and prices are low. It seems ironic that it is possible to purchase a flacon dating back thousands of years for the price of a modern bottle of perfume.

Pomanders & vinaigrettes

Perfume was reintroduced to Europe in the Middle Ages by the returning Crusaders, and, as trade routes with the East expanded, the art of perfumery flourished once more in the West. Scented oils and herbs were not just valued for their cosmetic purposes. Pomanders hung from the body or held in the hand were believed to protect against pestilence, and doctors treating plague victims even wore false noses impregnated with perfume, their bizarre "beaky" appearance possibly giving rise to the word "quack". By the 18thC the plague had retreated, and the pomander had been replaced by the vinaigrette, a tiny box containing a sponge soaked with aromatic vinegar, sniffed to counter unpleasant odours and fainting fits. In the 19thC no dressing table was complete without its bottle of smelling salts.

▶Pomander

The word pomander comes from the French *pomme d'ambre* ("apple of amber") or ambergris, a pungent secretion of the sperm whale, much used in perfumery. In their simplest forms pomanders were either oranges stuffed with cloves and held in the hand, or balls of solid scent and spices. These were housed in silver cases, which were worn round the neck as pendants or suspended from the waist on chatelaines or girdles. Some containers were perforated, others, like the example shown top right, snapped open for a reviving sniff. Though decorative, pomanders were primarily practical and protective.

Engraved silver pomander in the shape of a nut, ht 5.5cm (2¼in), German, late 17thC, **$825–990**

▼Memento mori

Pomanders came in many forms. Some incorporated as many as 16 compartments, opening out like the segments of an orange, each one containing a different scented oil or spice. This silver pomander is modeled as a skull, and opens to reveal three separate sections for solid perfume. Memento mori jewelry was worn by both men and women in the 16th and 17thC as a general reminder of the transience of life. The skull shape makes this pomander particularly valuable.

Silver pomander in the form of a skull, ht 2.5cm (1in), German, c.1700, **$2,475–2,970**

Carved nut vinaigrette with ivory pierced grill, c.1820, $82–132

Silver vinaigrette, made in London, c.1840, $264–297

The power of perfume
Perfumes were claimed to cure everything from smallpox to impotence. Hungary Water, created in the 14thC and a popular plague cure, was supposed to have made the 70-year-old Queen Elizabeth of Hungary so lovely that she was instantly proposed to by the King of Poland. The power of perfume could also be dangerous. Catherine de' Medici was rumoured to have poisoned one rival with a pair of scented gloves and another with an infected perfume burner.

◀ Vinaigrettes

The pomander was superseded by the vinaigrette, popular in the 18thC and 19thC. The plain silver box (above right), only 2.5cm (1in) long, has a pierced grille, which would have concealed its tiny sponge soaked with aromatic vinegar. Interiors were gilded to protect the metal from corrosion, and grilles were often beautifully decorated; this example has a grape pattern. Ladies liked to keep their vinaigrettes literally to hand, tucked inside a glove or carried in a muff or beaded purse. For this reason vinaigrettes tended to be small. The one concealed in a nut (above left) measures 3cm (1¼in) in length. Often made out of inexpensive materials, such as wood or bone, these miniature novelties are very sought after by collectors.

Rectangular clear-glass smelling-salt bottle with silver-gilt mounts and a vinaigrette compartment at one end, ht 5cm (2in) by Sampson Mordan & Co., London, 1873, $775–858

▼ Smelling bottle

The clear-glass smelling bottle on the left is still filled with smelling salts, and has a hinged lid with a spring-loaded fastener, so that the top could be popped open for instant access. The silver end contains a vinaigrette compartment. Vinaigrettes were incorporated into both smelling and scent bottles (see pp.24–5). Smelling salts (carbonate of ammonia), sometimes scented with lavender or rosemary, were purchased over the counter from chemists' shops. They were supplied in cheap glass bottles, often with the name of the manufacturer molded on the side, but ladies would decant the contents into their personal bottles.

Ceramics

Though perfume was still valued for its prophylactic powers, by the 18thC it was above all used for pleasure. The beauties of the period revelled in artificial aids. Smallpox scars were covered with decorative patches, cheeks were reddened with Spanish rouge, and complexions poisonously whitened with lead. Perfumes were crucial to an elegant toilette, concealing a lack of washing. Fashions were led by France, where Versailles was known as *la cour parfumée* and Mme de Pompadour spent half a million *livres* a year on perfume, popularizing flowery fragrances and elegant bottles. The French court purchased perfume flasks from Sèvres and St Cloud. In Britain rococo porcelain bottles were made at Chelsea, and, by the end of the century, Wedgwood was producing jasper-ware flasks in the Neo-classical style. Ceramic bottles remained popular throughout the Victorian and Edwardian periods, appearing in every shape and style.

Chelsea bottle with floral decoration and gold, c.1760, **$1,815–2,310**

▼Rococo toy

This rare Chelsea bottle, encrusted with raised floral decoration and painted with a bird on a branch, is mounted in gold with a stopper modeled in the form of a bunch of flowers. The Chelsea factory was founded in London in 1745 by Nicholas Sprimont, a Huguenot silversmith from Liège. Wares were aimed at "the Quality and the Gentry" and the factory specialized in luxury porcelain, in particular "toys", small decorative items including scent flasks. Chelsea scent bottles came in a variety of forms, often modeled as animals or figures, and are highly sought after today.

▶Neo-classical designs

Around 1774 Josiah Wedgwood introduced jasper ware: a hard, fine-grained and unglazed stoneware, used for a range of decorative items including perfume bottles. Inspired by the antique cameo, ceramics were stained (cobalt blue being a favourite shade), and applied with white relief decoration showing Classical figures and portrait reliefs. "The smelling bottles ... are very good and pretty things, particularly that with the festoon border of which I would have the rest made," wrote Josiah Wedgwood to his son in 1788. "You need not make any stoppers to the bottles, they use cork ones!"

Wedgwood jasper-ware bottle with silver screw top, early 19thC, **$577–742**

Porcelain bottle in the rococo style, with gilt-metal top and cork stopper, German, 19thC, **$660–825**

Porcelain baby bottle, attributed to Samson, but unmarked, 19thC, **$990–1,155**

▲▶ 18th-century revival

The 19thC saw a rococo revival, and porcelain bottles were reproduced in this style – most famously by the Paris firm of Edme Samson et Cie (est.1845). Samson specialized in manufacturing good-quality copies of 18thC designs. They were sold as reproductions, marked with the letter S. This inscription could be easily removed, however, and Samson pieces have been sold as period originals. Today they are collectible in their own right, and, ironically, Samson's own S mark is sometimes faked. Pieces are often attributed to Samson irrespective of maker, but 18thC-style bottles were produced by 19thC manufacturers across Europe.

▶ Floral decoration

Flowers were among the most popular forms of decoration on 19thC scent bottles. This stopperless bottle has the Royal Worcester factory mark on the back. Royal Worcester specialized in the production of shield-shaped flasks made from white and ivory porcelain. Surfaces were hand painted with flowers, their delicate colors mirroring the pastel tones favoured in contemporary ladies' fashions. Sometimes the decoration is signed. These bottles came with corks or pull-stoppers, many of which have long since been lost.

Royal Worcester porcelain bottle, factory mark on back, 1890s, **$214–264**

Silver

Silver was a popular material for scent bottles. Silver bottles were suspended from chatelaines and brooches. Silver-topped flasks were included in nécessaires, along with ear scoops, writing tablets, sewing materials, and other accessories deemed necessary in polite society. In the late 17thC the fashion developed for magnificent toilet sets in silver or silver gilt, often a wedding gift from husband to wife. These could number as many as 20 to 30 pieces, and reflected the growing popularity of cosmetics and perfumes, which were often liberally applied, and whose overuse was satirized by the writers of the time. Throughout the 18thC, vanity sets were luxury items, but by the Victorian era they were being mass-produced. While solid silver fittings remained exclusive and expensive, pressed glass and electro-plated silver mounts made perfume bottles and other dressing-table accessories available to a far wider market.

▶ **Portable perfume**
This pear-shaped bottle has a screw top and was designed to be hung from a chatelaine. These ornamental clasps were worn suspended from the belt, and carried a variety of items hung on short chains, including keys, watch, and scissors, the everyday necessities that we would keep in a handbag. Chatelaines were popular in Britain from the 17thC to the 19thC, though by the Victorian period they were no longer fashionable as jewelry but were worn as purely functional items by the housekeeper rather than by her mistress.

Silver engraved and molded scent bottle, possibly German, late 17thC, $412–495

Tortoiseshell nécessaire with silver fittings, 18thC, $1,402–1,567

▼ **Nécessaire**
Measuring only 7cm (2¾in) high, the miniature travelling nécessaire below dates from the 18thC. The box is made from tortoiseshell decorated with tiny silver nails, and the lid is inset with a mirror. The fittings include a tiny knife, an ivory writing tablet, silver tweezers, a bodkin with an ear scoop end, and a miniature silver-topped glass scent bottle. These luxury items really seem to capture the spirit of their period. This piece is in fine condition, and its contents are complete.

▼Solid silver

The heavy embossed silver perfume bottle shown below has a flip top and elegant repoussé work and may have been produced for a toilet set. Major manufacturers of the period include firms such as Asprey's, Mappin & Webb, and Walker & Hall, who supplied a wealthy clientele with handsome wooden boxes, lined with velvet and silk and filled with silver accessories. The cartouche seen here is blank. Some collectors are put off by the presence of a monogram, though if an item belonged to a figure of some importance or interest, a crest or monogram can enhance its value.

Silver dressing-table bottle, hallmarked London 1883, **$577–660**

▼Continental silver

The marks show that this silver mandolin (below left) was made in The Netherlands. The front has silver strings; the back is embossed with cherubs. Though the piece is large (l. 11.5cm/4½in) it holds only a minimal amount of perfume. The actual bottle is contained in the top of the instrument; it measures only about 2cm (¾in) in length and is opened with the ring-topped pull stopper. The cloisonné enamel-on-silver bottle (below right) has Russian marks on its base. Russian enamel ware is highly sought after, hence the price range of this item.

Enamel bottle with silver mounts, Russian, c.1900, **$1,402–1,567**

Silver scent bottle in the form of a mandolin, Dutch, 19thC, **$726–792**

Silver marks

Marks can be decoded with the help of a silver book and an eye-glass. Most British silver has four basic marks:

• The hallmark or town mark: the stamp of the assay office where the quality of the metal is tested. This is the first mark that should be identified in order to decode the date letter.

• The standard or quality mark indicating the standard of silver – sterling silver bears the lion passant; Britannia silver, higher in quality, the device of Britannia. Sometimes this mark can appear before the hallmark.

• The annual date letter, showing the year in which the object was hallmarked. Each assay office allocates its own specific letter to a year. Both the letter and the shield enclosing it are distinctive in form, enabling the piece to be dated precisely.

• The maker or sponsor's mark – the initials or symbol of the maker or retailer who sponsored the article when it was sent for assay.

The above marks are the most common; additional marks may be found. Foreign silver tends to be less systematically marked, but nationality can often be identified.

Clear glass

Perhaps the most typical 19thC perfume bottle is the cut-glass, silver-topped flask, produced in vast numbers for toilet sets, and found in many antiques shops today. Though the Victorian dressing-table was covered with bottles and pots, pungent perfumes, like cosmetics, were considered inappropriate for ladies. "Scent was much used by dandies on their hair and by women of bad reputation," recalled the writer Violet Wyndham, a child at the turn of the century. "Ladies seldom wore anything stronger than lavender water or that rather mysterious and unpleasant scent known as orris root." Etiquette books recommended simple floral scents and subtle application. "A refined woman will always reject odours which are too strong", advised Lady Colin Campbell in *The Lady's Dressing Room* (1892).

English cut-glass bottle with embossed silver flip top, late 19thC, **$247–330**

◀ Cut crystal

English lead crystal lent itself perfectly to the fashion for cut-glass vessels. Large spherical bottles were popular in the late Victorian and Edwardian periods, their surfaces carved in a variety of patterns. The bottle on the left is a fine example, and would been produced for a comparatively expensive toilet set. Cut crystal can be quite easily distinguished from press-molded glass, which provided a cheaper alternative. Crystal is brighter and heavier in weight; the cut edges are sharp to the touch, and the glass rings when tapped with the fingernail.

◀ Affordable bottles

By the turn of the 19thC, toilet sets were being mass-produced, major centers of manufacture including London, Sheffield, and Birmingham. Glass perfume bottles were made both as part of these vanity sets and independently, and were targeted at every level of the market: silver and crystal for the lady, brass and press-molded glass for the lady's maid. In their day, the simpler bottles would only have cost a few pennies each, and they remain affordable today, with prices beginning at under $80.

Left to right: cut-glass dressing-table bottle with silver collar and faceted stopper, c.1900, **$66–82**; miniature cut glass bottle, ht 4cm/1½in, with a brass flip top, c.1900, **$41–49**

Victorian glass bottle with brass screw top, **$132–148**

▲ Lay-down flask

The molded-glass bottle above is decorated with diamond facets and has a brass screw top concealing a cork. It is known as a "lay down" (designed to lie flat on the dressing-table). Its height (10cm/4in) suggests that it would have been used for eau de Cologne and other types of toilet water. Similar designs can also be found in colored glass.

▼ Symbolic shapes

Modeled on the horn of plenty, horn-shaped bottles were a Victorian favourite and were often suspended from finger rings (below left). Shoes or boots were popular as tokens of love and good luck; the custom survives in the tying of shoes onto the cars of newlyweds. Tiny shoes were made in materials ranging from wood to metal, serving as everything from pin-cushions to spirit measures or, as shown below right, a scent bottle.

Left to right: cut-glass horn-shaped bottle with silver mounts, l. 9cm (3½in), 19thC, **$231–280**; pressed-glass boot-shaped bottle, l. 6cm (2¼in), English, 19thC, **$132–165**

Stoppers

Ladies often used the frosted glass ends of stoppers to apply perfume, and by the 20thC, long, narrow, glass rods called daubers were often fused to the stoppers. Stoppers are particularly vulnerable to breakage and should be examined for damage and to ensure that they are original to the bottles. Also check the necks of the bottles for internal chips. Sometimes the stopper and base of a bottle are engraved with the same number, proving that they match.

▼ Travelling case

These two silver-topped, plain glass bottles are fitted in a shagreen travelling case (below left). Ladies either mixed their own perfume or purchased scent from the perfumer in simple, undecorated bottles. They then decanted it into their own personal bottles, hence the silver funnel in the central section, used to fill the vials. Another piece of essential equipment was a miniature corkscrew used for drawing the tiny corks out of scent bottles (below). Such items are also popular with corkscrew collectors, which increases their value.

Left to right: shagreen travelling case containing two silver-topped bottles and a silver funnel, 19thC, **$462–528**; ivory-handled miniature corkscrew, c. 1830, **$247–330**

Colored glass

Colored glass was used for perfume bottles not only for its decorative qualities but also because it protected the perfume from deterioration through exposure to light. By the 18thC, handsome colored-glass scent vials were being produced in Bristol, Stourbridge, and other major glassmaking centers. The 19thC renaissance in cameo glass was spearheaded by Thomas Webb & Sons. The expansion of tourism in the 19thC was an important influence on British manufacturers; perfume bottles were among the souvenir items made for a new generation of middle-class travellers. Scent flasks were also imported from Europe, in particular from Bohemia. Colored perfume bottles are among the most collectible in the field, with value depending on rarity, quality, and technique.

◄ Disposable bottles

These containers are known as "attar bottles", "throwaways", or "teardrops", and also as "Oxford lavenders". Made in Bohemia and England, they came in plain and colored glass, decorated with hand-painted enameling. They were purchased over the counter from the chemist or perfumer, and often thrown away once empty, hence their nickname. These charmingly naive bottles could be picked up 20 years ago for as little as $8 each. Today they cost far more, prices depending on color and decoration.

Green glass bottle, enameled and gilded with a gold screw top, late 18thC, **$660–825**

Three throwaways, early 19thC, clear and colored glass with hand-painted decoration and gilding, **$82–198** each

◄ Costly flasks

Dating from the late 18thC, this oval-shaped green glass bottle was probably made in Bristol and decorated in London. The Bristol glass houses specialized in the production of colored glass (in particular blue and green), so much so that the term "Bristol glass" has become generic for much of the colored-glass wares of the period, irrespective of place of production. Emerald-green glass was created by the addition of copper oxide, and blue glass by mixing cobalt with copper. These dark colors provided a perfect surface for painted decoration; popular designs included floral patterns and delicate rococo scenes.

Opaline glass bottle with silver mounts and finger ring, 19thC, **$363–396**

▲▶Ring bottles

Ring bottles were a Victorian favourite, used at balls and other public occasions. The bottle was worn suspended from a finger ring and clasped in the hand. An added advantage was that the scent was warmed, and thus emitted an even stronger fragrance when opened. The green bottle above is opaline glass, made opaque by adding bone ash and colored with metallic oxides. This was a practical choice, since opaline glass is less likely to show fingerprints than clear crystal. On the blue double bottle (above right) the gilding is slightly worn, presumably from being held in the warm palm of its Victorian owner.

Blue double bottle with gilded decoration, brass flip top, and finger chain, 19thC, **$412–462**

Stourbridge bottle, speckled in silver and gold, with silver screw top, 19thC, **$396–462**

▼Speckled glass

Glassware of this type was produced in Stourbridge, near Worcester. Molten glass, still hot on the punty rod, was rolled on flecks of enamel which were then absorbed into the glass, giving the final object a flecked or mottled appearance. The glass bottle seen here is speckled with silver and gold, and its conical shape is typical of lay-down bottles of the period (see p.19).

Souvenir bottles

The foiled-glass flask below was produced in Venice, and its style is typical of scent bottles manufactured for the 19thC tourist market. Also known as aventurine, the glass is flecked throughout with sparkling metallic particles, and was a speciality of the Murano glassmakers. The term aventurine is said to derive from the Italian word for chance, and according to legend this decorative process was discovered by accident. Confusingly, the word aventurina also describes a type of quartz, similar in appearance to this glass. This bottle still retains its cork and glass bead stopper; these beads are often broken off.

Venetian foiled-glass bottle with a brass flip top and mounts, **$264–297**

Spiral glass

Many different techniques were used for the decoration of scent bottles. The bottles shown below are made from spiral glass (also known as *vetro a fili*), a clear glass embedded with threads of opaque white and colored glass. These threads do not cross each other, but spiral up the glass in parallel lines. This technique was a speciality of Venice, where many bottles were also produced in *latticinio* glass: clear glass embedded with opaque glass threads forming complex lacy patterns.

Bohemian glass

The glass factories of Bohemia produced some of the most opulent perfume bottles of the 19thC. Their great speciality was colored glass, and ruby red was a Victorian favorite. The rich color was said to be obtained by a gold coin or ring being thrown into the molten glass. Early ruby glass was indeed made with a solution of real gold, but by the 19thC glassmakers were using particles of copper. A popular technique was flashing: clear glass would be dipped in the ruby glass, which made a thin outer coating that could be engraved to show the color beneath. This bottle is richly gilded, and both flask and stopper are marked with the same number.

Bohemian ruby glass toilet-water bottle with gilded decoration, **$247–289**

Left to right: pink-and-blue spiral glass with silver screw top; blue spiral glass with brass flip top, both c.1880, **$330–495** each

▼Cameo glass

Founded in 1837, the glass company of Thomas Webb & Sons is best known for cameo glass. This is composed of two or more layers of glass, the surface carved on a wheel or acid-etched to leave a design in relief. Webb employed two celebrated cameo artists, Thomas Woodall and George Woodall. Designs ranged from tear-shaped bottles to flasks in the form of swans' heads. Pieces were finely detailed and high in quality. Prices for Webb's cameo bottles have risen sharply. One of his most unusual designs, a flacon modeled as an alligator's head, can now fetch in the region of $16,500. Decorated with flowers, with a butterfly on the reverse, this tear-shaped flask is less dramatic but still a very desirable piece.

▼Heavy glass

This waisted bottle (below left) is made from overlay or cased glass. Inside an outer casing of glass, a second layer of a different color was blown. The object was then heated to fuse the layers, and the surface cut to reveal the contrasting tones beneath. Extremely heavy, the lemon-shaped bottle (below right) is made from thick opaline glass. A number of bottles were made in the shape of fruits (strawberries and nuts were favourite subjects), and this example is highly realistic.

Excise duties

At various times throughout history, taxes have been imposed on glass, in Britain perhaps most famously in connection with the Window Tax, which was first levied in 1691 and resulted in houses having their windows blocked. Duties according to weight of glass payable in 18thC Britain sent the British glass industry into decline and stimulated the development of heavy cut crystal in tax-free Ireland. When excise duties were at last repealed in 1845, manufacture of all types of glass flourished in Britain, and there was far greater experimentation with cased- and cameo-glass techniques, both of which used a large amount of materials.

Cameo scent bottle by Thomas Webb, silver mounts hallmarked London 1886, **$1,650–2,062**

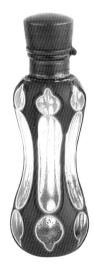

Blue-and clear-glass overlay bottle, with a brass flip top, mid-19thC, **$247–330**

Lemon-shaped bottle with silver screw top, English, 19thC, **$247–330**

Double-ended & dual-purpose bottles

With the end of the 18thC came the fashion for dual-purpose flasks, aristocratic fancies that concealed patch boxes, snuff containers, watches, and other favorite necessities. The double-ender is an archetypal 19thC bottle, and served both cosmetic and medicinal purposes. Tightly corseted Victorian women were subject to fainting fits, and double-ended bottles, which could be carried in reticules, contained flowery scents at one end, and at the other pungent smelling salts or a sponge soaked in aromatic vinegar, providing an instant remedy for fits of the vapours. Double-ended bottles are often extremely decorative, and prices vary, depending on color, quality of mounts, shape, and condition.

◀▼Dual-purpose bottles
Made from bright cut glass, these bottles served a double function. The brass-mounted flask on the left contains a miniature, retractable telescope. This bottle was used at the theatre and opera and is still in perfect working order. The bottle below conceals an engraved silver patch box. The underside of the lid is highly polished, and provided a mirror for ladies to check the application of their patches. The screw top is a Victorian replacement.

French combination scent bottle, cut glass with brass telescope and mounts, c.1800, **$1,115–1,320**

English combination scent bottle, bright cut glass with silver patch box and mounts, c.1780, **$990–1,155**

▼Double-ender
Though the whole bottle shown below feels smooth to the touch, double-enders were made by welding two separate bottles together. The end intended for scent has a screw top which opens to reveal a ground-glass stopper. The smelling-salt compartment has a snap top, opening at the press of the button in the neck. Under the cap, a glass disk provides a tight seal, thus ensuring that the volatile fumes of the smelling salts could not escape. Bottles came in clear and colored glass; sometimes each end was a different color. They were mounted in silver and brass, and makers' names or marks can sometimes be found inside the lids, as here, with the hallmark on the mount.

Green doubled-ended bottle with silver-gilt chased mounts, hallmarked Sampson Mordan London 1876, **$330–363**

▼Binocular bottle

This bottle held scent at one end and salts at the other. It snaps open to create an opera-glass shape and to reveal a vinaigrette concealed in the middle section. These central compartments also housed pillboxes or lockets. The maker, Sampson Mordan, was a British firm (established c.1813) that specialized in small decorative silverware, producing a large number of perfume bottles in the 19thC. Pieces by this manufacturer are very sought after today.

▼Novelty shapes

Though the classic cylindrical design is the most typical, double-ended flacons came in many forms and sizes. Measuring only 4cm (1½in) long, the blue, double-ended bottle below is barrel-shaped and decorated with diamond facets. Hung from a ring, the green double-ender (below right) with richly embossed silver mounts is most unusual. It is shaped like the barrel of a cannon, one end holding perfume, the other a vinaigrette, and carries the registration mark for 1875. Rare designs such as this will normally command relatively high prices.

Binocular double-ended scent bottle by Sampson Mordan, c.1880, **$792–858**

Novelty bottle in the shape of a cannon, 1875, **$792–858**

Blue, faceted, barrel-shaped and double-ended scent bottle, c.1880, **$297–330**

Novelties & miniatures

Portable scents provided an effective counter to unpleasant and unhygienic odours. Tiny glass bottles were attached to necklaces and brooches, and even earrings. With vials being both worn as jewelry and used as dressing-table bottles, there was a continual demand for novelty. Bottles were sculpted from every conceivable material, from semi-precious stones to nuts. Manufacturers patented their more unusual designs, and flasks were created in an almost limitless variety of shapes. One of the most curious fashions was for *pisseurs au parfum*, ceramic perfume sprinklers in the form of half-naked figures that sprayed scent from a tiny hole concealed in their private parts. Most manufacturers opted for less risqué designs, and novelty bottles were targeted at every level of the market.

▼▶ Stone and crystal

The perfume bottle on the right is made from Derbyshire Blue John, a type of fluorspar (crystalline mineral). Flasks of this type also served as hand coolers. The bottle below is carved from rock crystal. This was often used for flacons, because crystal is cold to the touch, thus preserving the freshness of its contents. Both bottles have cork stoppers with glass bead tops.

Derbyshire Blue John egg-shaped bottle, early 19thC, **$214–247**

Small rock-crystal bottle (h. 4cm/ 1½in), 19thC, **$214–247**

▶ Pendant bottles

The tiny bottles on the right, measuring around 3cm (1¼in) each, were designed to be hung from necklaces. The ceramic acorn (top) dates from the late 19thC, as does the bottle carved out of a peach stone (center). This example is highly unusual and desirable as it has a stanhope top – look through the lens in the silver stopper, and a series of seaside views is revealed. The glass ring-shaped bottle (bottom) has a silver screw top covering the original glass stopper. Sometimes ring bottles have magnifying glasses in the central holes.

From top to bottom: ceramic acorn with brass screw top, **$165–198**; peach stone bottle with silver stanhope top, **$297–330**; glass ring bottle, c.1830 **$181–214**

Left to right: Victorian mother-of-pearl bottle with a pull stopper, mounted in brass and suspended from a pierced-brass brooch decorated with cut-glass stones, **$330–412**; modern copy, no value.

◄ Real or fake?

Both the bottles shown above are made from mother-of-pearl. The example on the left, suspended from a brooch, is a 19thC original, while the flask attached to a finger ring, on the right, is a modern forgery. Mother-of-pearl was much used by the Victorians for jewelry and decorative items, but their designs have been copied. On reproduction pieces the shell surface tends to be less iridescent, flatter, and whiter in color than that found on an antique piece. Beware of brass fittings that are too shiny, and look out for touches of glue where the object has been crudely stuck to its mounts.

◄ Patented designs

The bottles on the right both have registration numbers, showing that their designs have been patented. The brass post box (top) has a diamond registration mark on the base. The hexagonal pillar box that this bottle commemorates was designed by the architect J. W. Penfold and made between 1866 and 1879. The porcelain walnut-shaped bottle (bottom) was made by Royal Worcester. The shell is painted with the registration mark R.No.28709, which means that this particular design was patented in 1885, and the silver top is hallmarked Sampson Mordan.

Top to bottom: brass post-box bottle, 1870s, **$115–148**; Royal Worcester porcelain walnut bottle with silver mounts, c. 1885, **$388–437**

Art Nouveau & Edwardian

The end of the 19thC saw the emergence of the commercial perfume industry as we know it today. Rather than making their own scents or decanting bought perfumes into their own flasks, women began buying pre-packaged, named brands over the counter. Perfumers such as Coty, Piver, and Roger & Gallet commissioned designs from well-known artists, and glass flasks from leading makers, including Baccarat and Lalique. France led the fragrance industry, and perfumers from other countries often adopted French names and ordered bottles from French makers. Boxes, once disposable, were now designed to complement the perfume and to be kept. Manufacturers soon recognized the importance of the flacon as a marketing tool and pioneered the concept of combining perfume, name, label, bottle, and box to create a seductive product.

◀ Metal overlay

The company of L.T. Piver had its roots in the 18thC when a family member opened a shop in Paris supplying perfumed gloves to the aristocracy. Piver was one of the first major fragrance manufacturers to develop elaborate and often luxurious packaging for its products. The flask for "Astris", shown on the left, with its beautifully faceted stopper, was created by Baccarat, and, rather than having a paper label, the bottle has a decorative bronze overlay with a central medallion inscribed with the perfume's name.

"Astris" by L.T. Piver in a Baccarat crystal bottle with metal casing, c.1910, **$148–165**

▼ Distinctive stoppers

The bottles shown below were produced by the Crown Perfumery Company, established in London in 1872. The firm made its name with lavender-scented smelling salts, and then moved into fine fragrances with such popular perfumes as "Crab Apple Blossom". The company also expanded into other areas: it produced toothpaste for Queen Victoria, and pioneered the idea of the air freshener. Bottles are immediately identifiable, due to their distinctive crown-shaped stoppers.

Left to right: green glass smelling-salt bottle and scent bottle, by Crown Perfumery, c.1900, **$33–58 each**

▼ Art Nouveau style

The rare flacon shown below was created by Louis Chalon for Roger & Gallet. The perfume was called "Bouquet Nouveau", and Chalon was a leading sculptor whose works were much admired at the Paris Exposition of 1900. The molded glass seems almost to pour over the pierced and gilt-metal casing with its fluid, naturalistic decoration. Roger & Gallet's packaging reflected contemporary artistic fashions, and this bottle is a typical piece of Art Nouveau design.

"Bouquet Nouveau" by Roger & Gallet, glass with gilt-metal overlay, c.1900, **$2,475–4,125**

Acid-etched and stained-glass flacon by Dubarry, decorated with insects, c.1920, too rare to provide realistic price range

◄ Insect decoration

Despite its French-sounding name, Dubarry was a British company, based at 81 Brompton Road, London, and established in 1916 as the perfume and cosmetics branch of the less romantically titled Standard Tablet and Pill Company Ltd. Dubarry specialized in luxury presentations, commissioning designs from the French sculptor Julien Viard, and bottles from the Depinoix glassworks in Paris. The bottle above, with its unusual pattern of iridescent insects, was made by Depinoix. Glassmakers often supplied the same design, or a marginally modified one, to various perfumers, and this bottle, with slightly different shading, was also used by Parfums Caray.

Boxes

An original box greatly enhances the value of a perfume bottle. Boxes came in a wide range of materials: wood, leather, cardboard, metal, and later plastic. Some clearly bear the perfume's name; on others the inscription is discreet (check the interior) or even non-existent. Many boxes have been separated from their bottles, but collectors buy individual boxes both as works of art in their own right, and in the hopes of reuniting them with their original contents.

▼ Desirable boxes

Dralle, a German company, launched "Illusion" around 1911. The Hamburg-based firm exported widely. "The woman who uses Dralle finds herself in company with the most exclusive," boasted an American advertisement in 1913. The company produced handsome presentations, and what makes the piece shown below particularly desirable is its box, a gilt-metal basket with a heart-shaped padlock.

"Illusion" by Dralle, glass bottle with metal box, c.1911, **$82–99**

▼Pochette

D'Orsay was established at 17 rue de la Paix, Paris, in 1908. The German and Dutch founders of the company wanted a French name with a suitably glamorous image. Count Gabriel D'Orsay (1801–52) was an artist, wit, and dandy, renowned for his Adonis-like looks and opulent dress sense. The count's name was adopted by the company, and his portrait appeared on packaging – though claims that the perfume was made from his recipes were pure advertising. The bottle shown below still contains its perfume and comes in the original suede pochette.

"Chypre" by D'Orsay, c.1912, glass bottle in beaded suede pochette, **$82–99**

Art Nouveau-style bottle in frosted and shaded glass, maker and perfume company unknown, c.1910, **£140–160**

◄ ►Naturalistic decoration

Feminine and floral, Art Nouveau was a style well suited to perfume bottles. On the bottle shown top right, the use of naturalistic decoration has extended from the stopper onto the flacon itself. The glass is frosted, and the decoration picked out with dark shading, a typical design feature of the period, and a technique employed by numerous glass artists, including Lalique and Viard. This was clearly a costly piece; unfortunately, however, the label is too worn to read, and the base of the bottle is unmarked. "La Feuilleraie" (bottom right) was launched by Gueldy in 1913. The name is based on the French word feuille ("leaf") and is reflected in the design. The embossed label shows a windswept tree, and the stopper is decorated with a blue leaf pattern.

"La Feuilleraie", by Gueldy, c.1913, **$124–140**

Cleaning

Great care should be taken when cleaning bottles. Areas decorated with hand staining, gilding, or enameling should be gently wiped. Avoid scrubbing and using abrasive cleaners. Labels are crucial to value and can be damaged by water, perfume, and other liquids. They should also be kept out of strong light, to avoid fading. Sealed bottles should be left unopened, as the presence of the original perfume can enhance the value of a bottle.

▼Trademark wars

In 1911 the French perfumers Caron launched the fragrance "Narcisse Noir". The round bottle with its black, glass, floral stopper was produced by Brosse, a well-known French glass factory. Both the bottle and its contents were much imitated, which caused Caron to take legal action to protect their creation, and inspired other manufacturers to trademark both products and packaging. Caron also produced "Narcisse Blanc", which has a white opaque glass stopper and is rarer than the black version.

◄▼Dressing table atomizers

The atomizer shown below right is decorated with a handsome copper overlay in the Art Nouveau style, and is operated by a pump mechanism. The atomizer shown below left, still in its silk-lined presentation case, has a rubber bulb-and-tube system, the bulb encased in a crocheted silk cover. The glass bottle is luxuriously gilded and enameled in black and gold. New influences such as the Ballets Russes and the glamorous fashions of Paul Poiret filtered through to scent bottles, and manufacturers experimented with brilliant colors and exotic designs.

Above, left to right: "Narcisse Noir", by Caron, c.1911, large bottle **$165–198**; smaller bottle (3.8cm/1¼in), **$140–157**

Left to right: atomiser, gilded and enameled orange and black, in silk-lined presentation case, made in the USA by DeVilbiss, c.1920, **$330–370**; atomizer with silvered top and copper overlay, c.1900, **$330–412**

Lalique

René Lalique (1860–1945) began his career as a jeweler. He experimented with glass initially for use in jewelry, and then for its own sake, becoming the leading glass artist of his generation. Lalique's glass output ranged from car mascots to a glass fountain for the 1925 Paris Exhibition. In 1905 he opened his first shop, at 24 Place Vendôme. Three years later the perfumer François Coty moved in next door and commissioned his neighbour to produce glass labels for his perfume bottles. Thus began a famous partnership. Coty wanted to make luxury affordable, and Lalique developed new techniques of press-molding, enabling bottles to be mass-produced, then hand-finished. He favoured demi-crystal glass with a lower lead content than crystal, and used etching and staining for decoration. The Lalique company created flacons for an estimated 60 perfumers.

▶ Affordable luxury

"Offer a woman the best product you can make and present it in a perfect container ... ask a reasonable price for it, and you will have a commercial proposition such as the world has never seen," said Coty. Dating from around 1913, Coty's fragrance "Muguet" was contained in a comparatively simple bottle, the decoration restricted to the stained and molded stopper, and the gold embossed label. Both stopper and flask (right) are numbered 291. Control numbers appear on most Lalique bottles; they are a good way of checking that bottle and stopper match.

"Muguet" by Coty, c.1913, $577–660

▼ Dressing-table bottles

The dressing-table bottle below is known as "Fougères" ("fern"), after the stylized fronds covering bottle and stopper. The flask has a green patina and is decorated with two frosted-glass medallions (front and back), lined with gold leaf. Each side shows the bust portrait of a different woman. Signed "R. Lalique" and numbered 489, this bottle was not produced for a perfumer but was created by Lalique for retail from his own catalogue.

"Fougères" dressing-table bottle, 1912, $13,200 –16,500

▼Decorative stoppers

Large, decorative stoppers were a Lalique speciality. A favorite design was the crescent- or tiara-shaped stopper, sweeping down the sides of the flacon. Shown below is "Bouchon Cassis" (blackcurrant), one of a famous series of bottles, all named after their stoppers, the shapes of which were inspired by fruit and flowers. Others include "Bouchon Mures" (blackberries), "Bouchon Eucalyptus", and "Bouchon Fleurs de Pommier" (apple blossom). On this rare version the stopper is in clear and frosted glass, and the flacon is molded with vertical lines. "R. Lalique, no. 494" is engraved under the base.

▼Celebratory designs

Both these designs are by Marc Lalique, son of René, for Nina Ricci. They express a sense of exuberance after the privations of World War II. "Coeur Joie" ("joyous heart") dates from 1946 and was the fashion house's first major fragrance. The heart-shaped bottle, decorated with leaves and flowers, came in a box showing female figures and hearts, designed by the painter Christian Bérard. This new romantic mood found its consummation in "L'Air du Temps" ("spirit of the times"), launched in 1948. The famous flacon dates from 1951. It has a stopper in the form of doves, representing love and peace.

"Coeur Joie" by Nina Ricci, c. 1946, large bottle (ht 15cm/6in), **$660–742**; small bottle (ht 10cm/4in), **$297–330**

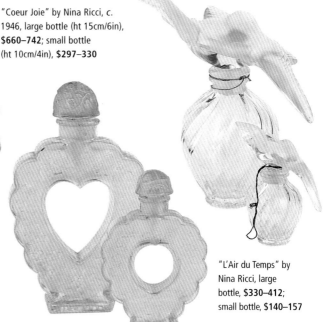

"Bouchon Cassis", c. 1929, **$9,900–11,550**

"L'Air du Temps" by Nina Ricci, large bottle, **$330–412**; small bottle, **$140–157**

Baccarat

Baccarat, one of France's most celebrated glass factories, was set up in 1764 in the town of the same name, under the patronage of Louis XV, to provide a national product that would stem imports of Bohemian glass. In the 19thC the firm produced high-quality crystal, and from the 1880s supplied fine bottles to the expanding perfume industry. Early clients included Houbigant, Guerlain, and Piver (*see* p.28). Competing with Lalique, Baccarat designed adventurous flasks and stoppers in the Art Nouveau style, and in the 1920s sculptor Georges Chevalier created a series of Art Deco masterpieces for the firm. In the 1930s bottles by Baccarat for Schiaparelli and Elizabeth Arden showed a new Surrealist influence, but World War II severely affected production, and though clients in the 1950s included Christian Dior, the golden age of the luxurious presentation was drawing to a close.

"L'Heure Bleue" by Guerlain, launched 1912, **$214–247**

▼**Guerlain**
Baccarat produced many bottles for Guerlain, one of the leading French perfume houses. This famous flacon, with its inverted, heart-shaped stopper, was created for Guerlain's classic fragrance "L'Heure Bleue", which was launched in 1912. The design was also used for "Fol Arôme" (1912) and "Mitsouko" (1919). Though Guerlain used the same flacons for decades, production was given to various factories, and the bases of bottles should always be checked for any identifying marks. This bottle (left) is acid-etched with the mark of the Baccarat factory.

▶**Luxury presentation**
This handsome crystal bottle (right) was created by Baccarat in 1928 for Houbigant's "Essence Rare". The blue velvet-lined box opens to reveal a luxuriously heavy flacon, faceted like a diamond. Founded in Paris in 1775, Houbigant was a highly prestigious perfumer whose clients included Mme de Pompadour, Napoleon, and the Imperial Russian court. A rare presentation such as this, complete with box and original perfume, would be very sought after by collectors.

"Essence Rare" by Houbigant, 1928, **$132–247**

"Nuit de Noël" by Caron, c.1922, **$124–140**

Identification
Baccarat bottles are often only identified by documentation and experience, since early examples were not always marked. Bottles were systematically engraved with a mark only from 1936. Prior to this, some were stamped, others had a round paper label, and many have no distinguishing mark.

▼Costly perfume
Jean Patou's "Joy" (1926), initially only available to his couture clients, was launched on the general market in 1930. It was proudly advertised as "the most expensive perfume in the world", a slogan coined by Patou's publicity agent, the socialite Elsa Maxwell. The costly fragrance contained over 100 ingredients, the principal essences being rose and jasmine. It needed a suitably stylish container, and Baccarat responded by creating this classically simple design.

▲Handbag bottle
Small portable flacons, elegant confections which could easily be carried in a handbag, were a popular accessory for fashion-conscious women in the 1920s. This bottle for Caron's "Nuit de Noël" was designed by Baccarat in 1922. The black glass from which the bottle is made reflects the name of the perfume. The *faux* sharkskin box is constructed from cardboard and has an extravagant silk tassel, a design that recalls a Japanese *inro*, or seal case.

"Joy" by Jean Patou, 1930s, **$198–231**

▼Victorian influence
Elizabeth Arden (1878–1966) was one of the 20thC's great names in cosmetics, owning over a hundred beauty salons in the USA and manufacturing countless products. Baccarat created this hand-shaped bottle (right) for "It's You", launched in 1939. Inspired by a Victorian posy vase but also echoing Surrealist motifs, the bottle came in various colours: clear, opaque white, or, as in this rare example, pink with blue details.

"It's You" by Arden, 1939, **$2,475–4,125**

1920s & 1930s

After World War I there was a desire for liberty and frivolity: women
abandoned their corsets, shortened their skirts, and bobbed their hair.
Wearing scent and cosmetics in public, like smoking and drinking,
became acceptable, and the perfume industry blossomed. Couturiers
added fragrance lines to their collections, and the competition between
fashion houses and perfumers sparked the creation of inventive bottles
in every style from Cubism to Surrealism, and in every material from the
finest crystal to affordable Bakelite. In 1921 Chanel "No.5" became the
first scent to bear the name of the designer, establishing a trend that
has been the economic mainstay of the fashion industry ever since.

**"No.5" by
Chanel, 1924,
$49–66
(with box)**

▲ Design classic
Chanel "No.5" was revolutionary in that it
combined both floral and synthetic substances
to provide a sophisticated contrast to the
predominately flowery fragrances of the early
20thC. It is thought that the great perfumer
Ernest Beaux gave Coco Chanel several mixtures
and she chose the fifth sample. Henceforth
"No.5" became her lucky number. This modern
fragrance demanded a chic container; simple
and square with an elegant black-and-white label
and clear graphics, the bottle epitomizes the
classic designs that have made Chanel famous.

▼ Family logo
"My Sin" was created by
Jeanne Lanvin (1867–1946).
At 13 Lanvin was apprenticed
to a dressmaker and by 18
she had opened her own Paris
workshop. Her only child,
Marie Blanche, born in 1897,
was a crucial influence on her
work. Maison Lanvin produced
clothes for women and girls,
and could dress a client
for life. The company logo,
designed by Paul Iribe and
still in use today, shows Lanvin
hand-in-hand with her
small daughter. The
distinctive ball-shaped
bottle was designed by
Albert Armand
Rateau.

**"My Sin" by
Lanvin, c.1925,
$132–165**

▶ Avant-garde design

Jean Patou was one of the most famous fashion designers of the 1920s, his style perfectly capturing the new liberated mood of the post-war years. He created a sensation by sending the tennis player Suzanne Lenglen onto the courts of Wimbledon in a sleeveless cardigan and a daringly short, knee-length skirt. He pioneered the sporting look for women's day wear, introduced suntan lotion, and was the first designer to monogram his clothes. Patou created many fragrances, most famously "Joy" (see p.35). "Colony", shown above right, was launched in 1937 after Patou's death. The distinctive pineapple-shaped bottle came in various sizes, with a gilded- or frosted-glass stopper.

"Colony" by Patou, 1937, **$577–660**

▼ Art Deco style

The elegant alabaster-and-gilt-bronze dressing-table set featured below comprises two crystal scent bottles and a glass trinket basket and is an archetypal Art Deco design. The finely modeled figures, whose gestures mirror a Classical pose, are trim, elegant, and streamlined. Their unabashed nudity is a perfect reflection of modern styling and the new freedom of the "Jazz Age".

Coco Chanel & "No.5"

"No elegance is possible without perfume," claimed Chanel. "It is the unseen, unforgettable, ultimate accessory of fashion." By the time of her death in 1971 the great designer had amassed a fortune from the famous "No.5". Celebrity enthusiasts have included such stars as Marilyn Monroe, who when asked what she wore in bed replied simply "Chanel No.5", causing sales to rocket.

▼ Portrait bottle

Hattie Carnegie was a leading New York fashion designer. She began producing fragrances in the 1920s, and from 1938 all her perfumes were sold in this bottle, conceived by Tommi Parzinger and manufactured by the Wheaton Glass Co. The bottle, said variously to be a portrait of Carnegie herself or of her niece, was also available in gilded glass.

Art Deco dressing-table set, c.1920s, **$660–825**

Portrait bottle by Carnegie, 1938, **$412–495**

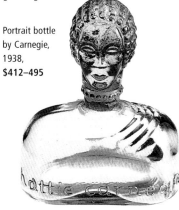

"Mon Studio" by Callisté,
c.1925, **$330–363**

▲Modernist simplicity

"Mon Studio" by the French
perfumers Callisté dates from
c.1925. The black glass bottle
reflects the move away from
flowing Art Nouveau lines
and floral decoration towards
simple geometrical shapes and
Art Deco styling. Black and
gold became very popular
colors for perfume
presentations during the
1920s. The nude on the label
is also typical of the period:
lean, athletic, with short hair,
and her body no longer semi-
concealed by the floating
drapery or cascading curls of
the Art Nouveau beauties.

▼Novelty shapes

Created by Corday, this
frosted-glass bottle is
modeled in the form of a
seated cat with a gilt metal
head. The company was
established in Paris in 1924
and named after Charlotte
Corday, who in 1793 stabbed
the French Revolutionary
journalist Jean-Paul Marat to
death in his bath and was
guillotined. Corday created a
wide range of novelty bottles,
many for export to the USA.

Cat bottle by Corday, 1920s,
$247–280

"June Roses" by Morny,
c.1922, **$33–49**

▲Traditional style

Morny was an English firm
established in 1910 and based
in Regent Street, London. To
convey the French image that
was so desirable in the
perfume market, and thus
boost foreign sales, the
company added a "de" in
front of its name. Although
"June Roses" has not been
found in catalogues before
1922, the bottle is traditional
in style and reflects the
influence of Art Nouveau,
which lingered on into the
1920s alongside the new Art
Deco styling. The bottle and
box seen here are in perfect
condition, and the perfume is
unused, making this very
much a collector's piece.

Price ranges for Czech glass reflect colour, complexity of design, and condition. Some shades, such as turquoise-blue and brown, are rarer than examples in clear glass and pastel tones. Bottles with figural stoppers are very desirable, as are unusual designs, such as horn-shaped flasks. Condition is another important factor; vulnerable areas include the bases of bottles and stoppers, as well as daubers or applicators, which were fused to the inner lid and frequently snapped off.

▲▶English favorites

Yardley is one of Britain's longest-established cosmetics and toiletry firms. It was founded in 1770 by Thomas Yardley, and became famous for scented soaps, "Old English Lavender Water", and other lavender-based products, for which it is still well known today. Yardley's scent "Freesia" came in an Art Nouveau-style box that pulled out like a drawer to reveal a decoratively molded bottle (above left). Handsome presentations such as this are far rarer than the smelling salts which Yardley also produced, which were commonly found in medicine cabinets and ladies' handbags. Dating from the 1930s, the bottle of lavender smelling salts shown above right has a typical Yardley label, adapted from a famous series of 18thC prints, *The Cries of London* by Francis Wheatley.

"Freesia" by Yardley, 1930s, **$33–49**

"Old English Lavender" smelling salts by Yardley, 1930s, **$8–10**

Pink Czech-glass dressing-table bottle, 1930s, **$132–198**

▼Czech glass

In the 1920s and 1930s, vast numbers of bottles and dressing-table sets were imported from Czechoslovakia. Typically, bottles are Art Deco in style, with cut decoration. Clear and frosted glass were both used, and sets often came in pastel colors (soft pink was a favorite shade). Great attention was paid to the stopper, which was elaborately decorated and could be perhaps three times as tall as the bottle itself. Czech glass was hugely popular in the USA, where comparatively simple flasks, such as the example on the left, retailed for as little as $1 a piece, and were marketed as affordable gift ware.

▼◀ Liberated designs

The shapes of perfume bottles during this period reflected women's new-found freedom. Many designs were based on the traditionally male preserves of smoking and drinking. Bristow's "Carnation" (a very rare English presentation shown below left) is shaped like an ashtray and comes complete with a cardboard cigarette. "Carnet de Bal" ("dance card"), by the Paris firm Revillon (below right), is in a brandy-glass-shaped bottle, designed to stand upside down on its stopper. Both bottles are unopened, which enhances their value.

▶ Regal style

Prince Matchabelli (1885–1935) escaped the Russian Revolution and came to New York, where in 1926 he established his own perfume company. Fragrances were given impressively regal titles, such as "Katherine the Great" and "Duchess of York". In 1927 Matchabelli patented the firm's famous crown-shaped bottle, based on his family crest. Bottles were produced both in clear glass and in a range of enameled colors, such as the blue crown (above, top), which is rarer and more desirable than the clear flask in front of it.

Left to right: crown-shaped bottles by Matchabelli, 1930s–1950s; blue enamel bottle, **$264–313**; clear glass bottle, **$124–157**

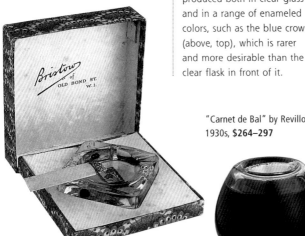

"Carnation" by Bristow, 1930s, **no price range available due to the rarity of this piece**

"Carnet de Bal" by Revillon, 1930s, **$264–297**

▲◀ Handbag scents

"A perfume needs to attract the eye as much as the nose," claimed François Coty, one of the great pioneers of perfume presentation. His fragrance "Paris" (c.1926) is presented in a small, white, metal travel case, designed to slip into the handbag (above). The same container was used for a number of different perfumes, and also came in enameled colors. The gilt metal bottle shown on the right was created for Coty's "L'Aimant". The word has two meanings, "magnet" and "loving", and the base of the bottle is shaped like a pair of pink painted lips (bottom right). The perfume's creator, Ernest Beaux, had worked for Coty but, according to legend, took his famous fragrance "No.5" (see pp.36–7) to Chanel because Coty claimed it was too costly to produce. Coty soon realized his mistake, trademarking the similar-smelling "L'Aimant" in 1928.

"Paris" by Coty, c.1926, **$198–231**

François Coty

Coty (1874–1934) was one of the founding fathers of the 20thC perfume industry. Born François Sporturno in Corsica, he founded his perfume company in Paris in 1900, using his mother's maiden name, which he later took for himself. The possessor of a great "nose", Coty devised new and spicy fragrances, pioneering the "Chypre" family of perfumes, based on oak moss. He was also a master salesman, not afraid to use unorthodox techniques. Early in Coty's career a famous Paris department store refused to take his new scent, "La Rose Jacquemimot". Coty responded by "accidentally" dropping the bottle on the floor, spilling the perfume. As the fragrance wafted through the shop, women crowded round demanding to buy it, forcing the emporium to stock Coty's product.

FACT FILE

"L'Aimant" by Coty, c.1928, **$91–107**

"Evening in Paris" was launched by Bourjois in 1928. During the 1930s it was the French company's best-selling line, particularly in the USA. The cobalt-blue bottle with its silver label, inspired by night-time Paris, was designed by French artist Jean Helleu, who also named the perfume. Bottles were housed in a variety of blue Bakelite boxes which played on the evening theme, ranging from a miniature hotel door, complete with his and her shoes left outside, to the blue owl and clock shown below, which snap open to reveal the miniature vial.

▼**Plastic fantasies**

The development of plastic and Bakelite meant that even lower-priced scents could be given fun and interesting packaging. "Mischief" was launched in 1935 by the British cosmetics company Saville, who created a whole range of moderately priced novelty presentations. In the example shown left, the glass flask fits inside the plastic top hat (which came in black, geen and white) and is packaged in a cardboard hat box inscribed "The latest thing in hats". In an alternative presentation for "Mischief", the bottle was housed in a dice-shaped plastic container, printed on each side with designs based on playing cards (below).

Top-hat container for "Mischief" by Saville, 1930s, **$181–214**

Dice container for "Mischief" by Saville, 1930s, **$132–165**

"Evening in Paris" by Bourjois, 1930s, **$214–247** each

"Dancing Time" by Dubarry,
c.1938, $132–165

▲Hollywood style

In the 1920s and 1930s the cinema had a major effect on the way women looked, with the great movie stars inspiring fashions in dress, hairstyles, and cosmetics. Film was also an important influence on the design of commercial scent bottles. "Dancing Time", created by the British firm of Dubarry, draws on the glamour of the Hollywood musical; the two ivory-colored plastic figures supporting the bottle suggest Fred Astaire and Ginger Rogers. Dubarry registered this design to prevent imitation. The packaging seen here still bears its original British price label.

▼Brosse glass

"Kobako" was first produced by Bourjois in 1936. The scent came in a Chinese-red Bakelite box (available in four sizes), simulating lacquer and decorated with peonies (below right). The frosted-and clear-glass flask, inspired by a Chinese snuff bottle, was produced by Brosse. Founded by E. Thirion in 1854, this French glass company adopted the name of Verreries Brosse around 1880. It made bottles for many major 20thC perfumers, from Caron and Houbigant in the early 1900s to Balenciaga and Dior in the 1950s. Its high-quality glassware is much prized by collectors.

FACT FILE

Bourjois

Founded in Paris in 1869, Bourjois began by producing theatrical makeup for clients such as Sarah Bernhardt. As the use of cosmetics became more generally acceptable, Bourjois exported worldwide and spearheaded new trends. The company pioneered the development of dry rouge and the powder compact, but its most famous product was the perfume "Evening in Paris", launched in 1928. Moderately priced, it combined Bulgarian rose, tuberose, and carnation. Above all, it was brilliantly named and packaged, evoking an image of Parisian glamour that proved irresistible to women around the world.

"Kobako" by Bourjois, c.1936, Brosse bottle in a Bakelite box, $495–660

Guerlain

Among the most enduring perfume dynasties is Guerlain. The firm was founded in 1828 by Pierre-François Pascal Guerlain, who made his name by concocting personalized perfumes for his customers and went on to become perfumer to the French court and to other European royal houses. Pierre-François died in 1864 and was succeeded by his sons Gabriel, who ran the business, and Aimé, who devised the scents, including "Jicky" (1889), which heralded the advent of modern perfumery. Aimé's nephew Jacques, one of the great "noses" of the 20thC, created "L'Heure Bleue" (1912), "Mitsouko" (1919), and "Shalimar" (1925), all still in production. Although it ceased to be a family-run business in 1996, Jean-Paul Guerlain is still the master perfumer of the house.

◄ **Imperial style**
"Eau de Cologne Imperiale" was created in 1853 for Eugénie, Empress of France and wife of Napoleon III. In accordance with 19thC fashions, which prohibited the use of strong perfumes, the scent was light and fresh, combining orange, lemon, and bergamot with lavender and rosemary. The bottle itself was decorated with a bee motif, the imperial emblem, and also gilded. Still in production today, this fragrance established Guerlain's position as perfumer to the French court.

"Eau de Cologne Imperiale", 20thC bottle, **$140–157**

▼ **Famous fragrances**
Conceived by Aimé Guerlain, "Jicky" was initially popular with men rather than women. Revolutionary in its day, it combined natural and synthetic fragrances, and used musk, ambergris, and civet to create a daringly spicy scent. Jicky was the nickname of Jacques Guerlain, Aimé's nephew and the creator of "L'Heure Bleue", a blend of Bulgarian rose, orris, and heliotrope with vanilla, jasmine, and musk. The "Jicky" bottle (far right) is not marked; the "L'Heure Bleue" bottle (right) is stamped "Cristal Nancy", a French maker that closed in 1934.

Left to right: "L'Heure Bleue", **$264–313**; "Jicky", **$124–140**

▼Japanese mystery

Measuring 20cm (8in) high, this clear-glass eau-de-toilette flacon with its frosted-glass stopper was used for a number of different fragrances. This particular bottle still contains "Mitsouko", named after the Japanese word for mystery. A pungent fragrance, combining jasmine, patchouli, bergamot, oakmoss, and peach, "Mitsouko" was the favorite perfume of Sergei Diaghilev, founder of the Ballets Russes.

"Mitsouko", launched 1919, $132–165

▼Asian influence

The East exerted a huge influence on artists and designers·in the first part of the 20thC, and this extended to perfume production. Named after the famous gardens created by the 17thC Indian ruler Shah Jahan for his wife Mumtaz Mahal, "Shalimar" includes sandalwood and patchouli. The Oriental-style flacon was produced initially by Baccarat (see pp.34–5), and later by other manufacturers. The bottle shown below is unmarked. A rival company launched a perfume also called "Shalimar", and a legal battle ensued, forcing Guerlain temporarily to replace the perfume's name with its stock number "No.90", as shown on the companion bottle.

From left to right: "No.90", $124–140; "Shalimar", $165–206

Guerlain vs Guerlain

The scents of Guerlain should not be confused with the products of Parisian perfumer Marcel Guerlain, who founded his own company in 1923 and produced fine, figurative bottles. The Guerlain family adopted the slogan *Nous n'avons pas de prenon* ("We have no first name") and brought a successful lawsuit against Marcel Guerlain, who changed his company name to the Société des Parfumeurs Français.

▼Deco design

The opaque glass bottle below was produced by Baccarat for Guerlain's "Liu" in 1929. Black and gold were favorite colors in Art Deco design, the influence of which can also be seen in the geometrical shape of the box and bottle. Containing jasmine, ylang ylang, and vanilla, the perfume was named after the slave girl in Puccini's opera *Turandot*, premiered in 1926.

"Liu", 1929, Baccarat bottle with box, $412–495

Schiaparelli

The Italian-born designer Elsa Schiaparelli (1890–1973) entered couture by accident in the mid-1920s, when friends commissioned copies of a sweater she had designed for herself. By 1930 her business was worth 120 million francs a year. Despite her financial success, Schiaparelli thought of herself first and foremost as an artist, introducing her passion for Surrealism into fashion and collaborating with Salvador Dali, Jean Cocteau, and Christian Bérard. For her braver clients, she created outfits out of cellophane, and hats shaped like lamb cutlets, and she was the first designer to exploit the decorative potential of the zip fastener (a daringly new accessory in the 1930s). Schiaparelli's perfume presentations were equally imaginative and witty. They drew on favorite Surrealist motifs, providing some of the most exciting, collectible designs in the history of commercial perfume bottles.

"Shocking",
1950s,
$412–495

◄ Shocking

Schiaparelli designed costumes for the actress Mae West, who could not come to Paris but sent the couturier a plaster statue of herself in the pose of Venus de Milo. West's silhouette inspired this bottle (left), created in 1936 by the artist Eleanore Fini for the perfume "Shocking". Covered with a glass dome, the flask is shaped like a dressmaker's dummy, with a tape measure round the neck and glass flowers at the head, an image combining the Victorian with the surreal. For the packaging Schiaparelli created a new color, Shocking Pink, later to become her trademark.

◄ More shocking?

"Zut" (1948–9) was one of the few Schiaparelli perfumes not to begin with the letter S. The bottle (right) is modeled as the lower half of a woman's body. Her star-covered skirt has slipped to the floor to reveal her gilded underwear: hence, perhaps, the title of the perfume, a mild French expletive. A green sash is tied round the waist. The bottle came in a matching green-and-gold box, secured by a silk garter, the perfect finishing touch for this daring presentation with its "Naughty Nineties" image.

"Zut", c.1948–9,
$577–660

Presentation set housing four
perfumes, c.1940s, **$206–247**

Left to right: "Sleeping", 1938,
candle bottle, **$297–330**;
candlestick bottle, **$495–577**

▲ Surrealist designs

Launched in 1938, "Sleeping"
came in a bottle designed by
Baccarat (see p.34) and shaped
like a candle, with a flame
stopper. It is shown above in
two versions, the larger (ht
21cm/8¼in) in the form of a
candlestick, the smaller a free-
standing candle (ht 15cm/6in).
Sleep and dreams were
important sources of inspiration
for the Surrealist artists who
formed part of Schiaparelli's
circle and contributed to her
work. "Sleeping" was presented
in a conical box, cool blue in
color and modeled in the
form of a candle snuffer.

▲ "S"

"To find the name of a
perfume is a very difficult
problem because every word
in the dictionary seems to
be registered," complained
Schiaparelli in her memoirs.
"The name had to begin with
an S because that was one of
my superstitions." Titles ranged
from "Silence" and "Spanking"
to a perfume simply called "S".
This Shocking Pink presentation
set (above) contains four
perfumes, including
"Shocking", "Sleeping", and
"Snuff". The label of the fourth
bottle is too worn to read. The
glass flacons each have long
glass daubers inside, for
applying the scent.

Miniatures, clockwise from top:
"Succès Fou", 1950s, **$330–412**;
"S", 1960s, **$33–49**; "Shocking",
1930s–1950s, **$33–49**

Le Roi Soleil

In 1946 Schiaparelli
produced one of the
most famous scent
bottles of all time, "Le
Roi Soleil", designed by
Salvador Dali and
produced by Baccarat.
The gilded stopper was
in the form of the sun,
with a face composed of
swallows, while the bottle
itself was ridged and
enameled to simulate
rocks and presented in a
gilded metal scallop
shell lined with satin.
Today this bottle could
be expected to fetch
$13,000 plus at auction.

▼ Miniatures

The three miniatures below
are "Shocking" (in torso-shaped
bottle), "S" (round bottle),
and "Succès Fou" (leaf-shaped
bottle). This last design was
created in 1953 especially for
this fragrance by Schiaparelli
and Marcel Brunhoff (Editor
in Chief of French *Vogue*), and
this particular miniature is
very rare, hence its value.

1940s & 1950s

For much of the 1940s, perfume production in Europe was curtailed by wartime restrictions, but peace and the end of rationing brought a surge in demand. New designers such as Christian Dior and Balenciaga launched sophisticated, elegant fragrances. The actress Audrey Hepburn advertised "Interdit" for Givenchy, while Dior commissioned limited-edition flasks for couture clients. At the same time, however, new technologies developed during the war stimulated mass production and the use of man-made materials. Glass stoppers were replaced with plastic screw tops, and fun designs provided a substitute for hand-crafted goods. As the labour market expanded, so a new generation of purchasers emerged: young women, with jobs, without children, and with money to spend on themselves.

"Miss Dior"
by Dior, 1950s,
$165–198

◀The New Look

"I designed clothes for flower-like women," claimed Christian Dior (1905–57) in his autobiography. "I brought back the neglected art of pleasing." Launched in 1947, Dior's New Look reintroduced a feminine, hourglass silhouette, emphasizing the bust, cinching the waist, and flouting austerity restrictions with long, flowing skirts.

Designers of the period often launched fragrances along with their latest lines, and "Miss Dior" (named after the couturier's sister) appeared in the same year as the New Look. The curvaceous lines of the bottle, created by Baccarat, mirrored Dior's dress designs. Its urn shape harked back to 18thC fashions, an important influence on the couturier's controlled and structured style.

▼Restrained elegance

Alongside Dior, the Spanish-born couturier Cristóbal Balenciaga (1895–1972) was perhaps the most influential designer of the 1950s. He was famous for his tailoring, seen in his box-shaped jackets, cut-away collars, and three-quarter-length sleeves, which freed the wrist for a dab of perfume. Balenciaga's "Quadrille" was introduced in 1952. Its elegant bottle was created by Brosse, while the white quilted box suggested luxurious fabric.

"Quadrille"
by Balenciaga,
1952,
$33–49

"Trésor" by Lancôme, 1952,
$264–313

Unopened bottles
The value of scent bottles is enhanced if they are unopened and still contain their original perfume, known as the "juice". Many bottles only look their best when filled with scent. The condition of the box, as well as that of tags, bows, labels, and any other elements attached to the flask, is also important. Collectors are prepared to pay a premium for presentations that appear factory fresh.

▲▶ Stylish shapes

Founded by Armand Petitjean in 1935 and named after a French château, Lancôme produced both cosmetics and fragrances. "Trésor" ("treasure"), above left, was created in 1952. The heavy crystal bottle, designed by Georges Delhomme, was cut to resemble a faceted diamond and originally came in a silken box. "Poivre" ("pepper") was launched by the firm Caron in 1955. The perfume was marketed in curiously dimpled bottles, which looked as though the glass was studded with peppercorns. The toilet-water bottle shown above right, with its glass rope handle, is pear-shaped, and is a visual pun on the similar-sounding words poivre and poire ("pear").

"Poivre" by Caron, 1955,
$280–330

"Cabochard" by Grès, 1959,
$124–140

▼ Riches to rags

In her youth Mme Grès (1910–93) wanted to become a sculptor, but, frustrated by poverty, she turned to dressmaking instead. From the 1930s she used silk jersey to create her famous draped dresses, Classical in influence and sculptural in style. The fragrance "Cabochard" ("headstrong") was launched in 1959. The monochrome design on the box, with its scratchy, graphic lines, is typical of 1950s styling. The perfume (chypre with a leather note) became a classic, but did not make the fortune of Mme Grès, who sold the rights and died, once again in poverty.

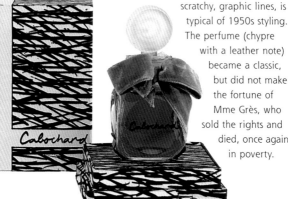

▼Fifties feline

The long-necked cat was a favorite decorative icon of the 1950s, appearing in every medium from patterns on textiles to pottery statuettes. The American cosmetics firm Max Factor used this velour-covered feline to hold several different scents: "Primitif", "Hypnotique", and, as here, "Electrique". Prices were low, and names exotic and foreign. These fun presentations were made from unashamedly artificial materials. Cats came with diamanté eyes and were variously decorated with pearl collars, spotted bow ties, plastic flower necklaces, and miniature feather boas. The perfume was presented under a plastic dome, in a whimsical interpretation of Victorian style.

▼Mirror bottle

Manufacturers used all sorts of presentations to make their bottles stand out. Marquay's "Prince Douka" toilet water (below) came complete with a mirror on one side of the bottle. Established in 1947, the French perfume company produced a number of witty designs. "Prince Douka" was also available in a figural bottle, representing an Indian maharajah with a jewelled satin cape, while for "Mr Marquay", a men's fragrance launched in the 1950s, Salvador Dalí created an asymmetric bottle capped with a plastic top hat and painted with moustaches.

▼Cheap and cheerful

In the 1950s, American dime stores and shops such as Woolworth's sold cheap and cheerful perfumes in bottles made from pressed glass and plastic. The fragrances might have been less than exclusive, but what these containers lacked in elegance they made up for in novelty design. Animal shapes were especially popular. Such bottles are still very affordable today, but be prepared to pay more if the bottle depicts a favorite cartoon character or if it is made of Bakelite.

Left to right: "Prince Douka" by Marquay, front and back, 1951, **$140–157**

"Electrique" by Max Factor, c.1954, **$33–41**

Clockwise from top left: "Jockey Club" cat with blue bow, c.1940s, **$16–25**; glass bird with Bakelite stand and stopper, 1940s, **$33–41**; clear glass mouse with tassel, 1950s, **$16–25**

▼ Plastic packaging

"Perfume O'Clock" by Stuart Products came in a glass bottle decorated with a clock face, set inside a plastic container shaped like a grandfather clock (below). When the perfume was gone the bottle could be removed, allowing the stand to serve as a holder for a fob watch. Founded in 1935, Stuart Products was based in St Paul, Minnesota. The firm specialized in novelty presentations, which retailed for as little as $1 a piece.

"Perfume O'Clock" by Stuart Products, 1940s, **$140–157**

▼ British bottles

Dating from the 1940s, this "Sweet Pea" scent (below) was made by Boots, the massive chain of British chemists' shops founded by Jesse Boot, who opened his first pharmacy in 1877. In the UK such items are commonplace, and their value is not high. However, in the USA the rarity factor comes into play. Boots is a sought-after name, and the bottle seen here could perhaps fetch as much as $60–80. Potter & Moore was another long-established British toiletries firm. The attraction of the bottle on the right lies not in the scent but in the plastic container with its picture of Goofy. The value is enhanced by the fact that it would appeal to both perfume-bottle and Disney collectors. Both bottles measure about 7cm (2¾in).

FACT FILE

Screw-top bottles

All the bottles on this page have screw tops, which were far cheaper to produce than ground-glass stoppers and more practical for smaller, portable flasks. To confirm the age of screw-top bottles, look inside the tops. Caps made before the 1960s tend to have inner linings of silver material, rubber, or cork. After this date, they are usually lined with plastic.

Left to right: "Sweet Pea" by Boots, 1940s, **$13–16**, and "Mitcham Violets" by Potter & Moore, c.1950, **$82–99**

Men's fragrances

From antiquity, scent has been used by men as well as women. In Tudor England men wore perfumed gloves and sniffed pomanders, and in the 17thC it was the fashion to sport wigs drenched with scented powder to ward off lice. An 18thC report states that "gentlemen will spend a whole morning in scenting their linen, dressing their hair and arching their eyebrows", and the Regency Period (c.1790–1830) is famous for such archetypal dandies as George "Beau" Brummel and the Prince Regent (later George IV); the latter's perfume bill in 1828 came to over £500. Victorian men were more restrained, sticking to simple colognes and hair oils, but after World War II the men's scent industry blossomed with the development of commercial aftershaves.

▼ Silver accessories

In the Edwardian period (1901–10), toilet sets often included silver accessories such as cologne bottles, shaving equipment, hair brushes, and sometimes curling tongs for the moustache. The glass cologne bottle below is housed in a satin-finished silver case made in the USA by the Gorham Manufacturing Co. The front of the bottle is marked "Cologne"; the back shows the former owner's monogram.

Leather travelling set, c.1920, $660–742

Men's cologne bottle in a silver case by Gorham, c.1906, $825–907

◄ Travelling sets

Men's toilet sets were often contained in fitted cases designed for travelling. Many were produced for officers in the armed forces, and, in the early 20thC for tourists taking advantage of the new-found freedom offered by the motor car. Men's perfume bottles tend to be less opulent in design than those for women, and the decoration, as on the set shown above left, is usually simple and restrained. This box contains three cologne bottles, all of which feature glass stoppers concealed within silver screw tops. The lid of the case is inscribed "Falize Orfèvre, 17 rue St Honoré, Paris", after either the maker or the retailer.

▼ Classic cologne

From the 18thC eau de Cologne was a dressing-table favorite with men as well as women. One of the most famous brands was "4711" made by the German firm of Rhinegold. The number "4711" was said to represent the code for the scent's secret formula, given to Wilhelm Mulhens, founder of the company, as a mysterious wedding gift in 1792; however, it may simply have been the street number of Mulhens's factory in Cologne. Whatever its origins "4711", with its distinctive gold label, became the best-selling eau de Cologne in the world.

"4711" eau de Cologne by Rhinegold, 1930s, **$33–41**

"Snuff" by Schiaparelli, 1940, **$247–330**

▲ Male fantasy

The pipe-shaped bottle above, with the plastic mouthpiece as the top of the flacon, was designed in 1940 by Elsa Schiaparelli (see pp.46–7) for her men's fragrance "Snuff". In keeping with the tobacco theme, the bottle was presented in a wooden cigar box. The image of the pipe was not only masculine but also recalled Surrealist paintings, most notably René Magritte's picture *Ceci n'est pas une pipe* ("This is not a pipe"). "Snuff" is one of the few flasks for men from the 1940s that can compete in terms of imaginative design and desirability with women's bottles of the same period.

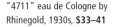

Eau de Cologne

Eau de Cologne is an aromatic blend of rosemary, neroli (orange flower), bergamot, and lemon oils. The Irish playwright Richard Sheridan drank it as a hangover cure, and the Emperor Napoleon was also a fan, even eating it on sugar cubes, as well as pouring it over his head and shoulders each day. He is said to have used 60 bottles a month, and to have commissioned a specially designed flacon that could be slipped inside his military boots.

▼ Macho marketing

To counteract any suggestion of effeminacy, many post-war aftershaves were given overtly masculine names and packaging. A typical example is Fabergé's "Brut 33" (left), advertised by the boxer Henry Cooper and one of the defining smells of the 1970s. Prices for these bottles are low, although current enthusiasm for the styles of the 1960s and 1970s could spark more interest.

Left to right: "Corvette Talc For Men", 1960s, **$20–23**; "Wild Country" by Avon, 1970s, **$13–16**; "Brut 33 Splash-On Lotion" by Fabergé, plastic bottle, 1970s, **$33–41**

1960s & 1970s

The 1960s and 1970s did not represent a golden age of bottle design. Fine perfumes, like couture clothes, traditionally sold to older women, but the emphasis was now on the youth market and cheaper products. London took over from Paris as the Mecca, of fashion with designers such as Mary Quant and Barbara Hulanicki at Biba introducing their own, affordable, fragrances. As flower power bloomed, interest grew in Eastern aromatic oils, supplied in anonymous bottles and worn, like jeans and long hair, by both sexes. While Avon ladies epitomized consumer culture, by the late 1970s the mood had changed, with the newly opened Body Shop offering natural, environmentally friendly products in refillable containers.

▼Trendy styles

The American company Fabergé (est.1936) targeted its perfume at a young audience. '"Fragrance à la Mood" (below) offered three different colognes, each helpfully inscribed with its own slogan: "*Aphrodisia* – my mood is sophisticated", "*Woodhue* – my mood is inquisitive", and "*Flambeau* – my mood is torchy". The box is decorated with photographs illustrating these different states of mind. The appeal of this presentation lies in its tongue-in-cheek humour and in its 1960s feel.

"Fragrance à la Mood" by Fabergé, 1960s, **$16–25**

▼▶Avon calling

Avon bottles can be a good starting-point for the collector. Very popular in the 1960s, they were mass-produced in a wide range of novelty styles. Avon scents can still be easily and cheaply picked up from flea markets and car-boot sales, but interest is growing, and rarer examples will fetch higher prices. Mint and boxed bottles are most sought after.

"Scent With Love" (tubular box containing "Bird Of Paradise" perfume in pen-shaped bottle) by Avon, 1960s, **$41–58**

Brown glass dog bottle by Avon, 1960s, **$8–16**

Left to right: avocado oil in small
bottle with rubber top, and bay
face oil (for men), both by Biba,
1970s, **$23–30** each

▶ Retro chic

The 1960s and 1970s saw a
revival of interest in Art
Nouveau and Deco styles, a
trend pioneered by Barbara
Hulanicki, founder of Biba.
Named after Hulanicki's sister,
Biba was a boutique for the
fashionable young, attracting
clients such as Twiggy and
Julie Christie as well as hordes
of teenage girls. The company
was established in 1964 and
sold clothes and other products
drawing on the designs of the
1920s and 1930s. In 1969,
Hulanicki introduced Biba
cosmetics; three years later
she opened her flagship store,
Big Biba, a massive Art Deco
extravaganza on London's
Kensington High Street.
Everything sold in the shop,
from perfume bottles to food,
was marketed in distinctive
black-and-gold packaging.
Biba went bankrupt in 1976,
and today its products are
increasingly sought after,
particularly by younger
collectors and seventies
enthusiasts. The bottles shown
above right were created for
scented oils.

◀▼ Perfume waxes

A seventies reinterpretation of
the pomander, perfume waxes
(solid perfumes concealed in
pieces of costume jewelry such
as necklaces and bracelets) are
a comparatively new area of
the collectors' market. Though
pieces can still be found
cheaply, perfume waxes are
attracting a growing number
of collectors, particularly in
the USA. Prices depend largely
on the maker, and pieces by
leading costume-jewelry
companies, such as Trifari,
are most desirable.

The story of Avon

In 1880s USA, a door-
to-door bible salesman,
David H. McConnell,
found that the perfume
sample offered free with
each purchase was more
popular than the books.
He set up the California
Perfume Company in
1886, recruiting women
to sell on the doorstep.
Business boomed, but
McConnell became
concerned that the
firm's trading name was
too regional. In 1939,
inspired by a visit to
Stratford-upon-Avon in
England, he changed
the company name to
Avon Products.

FACT FILE

"Intimate" perfume wax in gilt
pendant (chain not shown), 1970s,
$33–41

Owl perfume wax brooch by Avon
(open and closed), 1970s, **$16–20**

Miniatures

Miniatures are one of the fastest-growing areas of the perfume bottle market, and there are now specialist collectors' clubs around the world. Known as *echantillons* in France (a major center of both production and collecting), these tiny bottles were developed as testers or samples, allowing a client to try out a new perfume in the comfort of her own home. Bottles were distributed free, and were supplied as an added extra with the purchase of a full-size flask. They were also made for retail, often selling in boxed sets containing a variety of fragrances. Miniatures come in many forms, from simple glass test tubes to exact reductions of full-sized bottles. Value has nothing to do with size but everything to do with rarity. Some miniatures, such as the Guerlain bottle shown opposite, were produced only in very limited numbers, and are highly collectible.

▼**Boxed set**
"Ramage" ("bird song") was launched by the French company Bourjois (see p.43) in 1951. The boxed set below contains five miniatures, each glass vial still enveloped in its paper tag inscribed with the perfume's name and the words *Offert gratuitement* (free gift). It is very rare to find such a set unused and complete, hence the value of this one.

"Ramage" by Bourjois, boxed set of five samples, c.1951, **$132–165**

Left to right: "In Love" by Hartnell, 1950; "California Poppy" by Josephine Kell, 1940s; "Great Expectations" by Goya, 1950s, **$25–33** each

▲**Popular perfumes**
These British miniatures above, measuring under 5cm (2in) high, all have plastic screw tops and represent favorite scents of their day. "In Love" was launched in 1951 by the couturier Norman Hartnell (1901–79), while "California Poppy" inspired a craze for poppy designs in the 1930s and 1940s. "Great Expectations" is by Goya (est.1937), a firm specializing in handbag vials.

"English Rose Celebration" containing "Evergreen Cologne" by Peter Claridge, 1953, **$33–49**

Perfume cards
Rather than distributing sample bottles, perfume counters will often give out a presentation card sprayed with a fragrance. Collectors are interested in these not just for their smell (which tends to dissipate quickly) but also for their illustrations, graphics, and printed information. Such cards date back to the 19thC and can be found on sale at collectors' fairs.

▲▼Novelty miniatures
Miniature scents were often produced as souvenirs and gifts sets. In 1953, Peter Claridge created the patriotic package above to celebrate the coronation of Elizabeth II. Also seen here (below) is a miniature dating from the 1960s, whose presentation is the epitome of the cute gift pack. The tiny bottle of Lownds Pateman "Violet Perfume" is clasped in the arms of a brushed-nylon koala bear.

Lownds Pateman "Violet Perfume" by Michael Lownds in koala gift pack, 1960s, **$16–25**

"Mitsouko" sample by Guerlain, 1976, **$132–165**

Perfume vending machine, late 1930s, **$495–660**

▲Rarity value
Created by Guerlain (see pp.44–5) in 1976, the gift sample above contains 1ml of perfume. The flask is known as the Pagoda, after its green plastic stopper. Its unusual design was not popular with retailers, and it was withdrawn within the year. As a result it is extremely rare; although small (about 2.8cm/1in), examples fetch a high price. This bottle contains "Mitsouko"; the same design was used for "Shalimar" and other Guerlain perfumes.

▲Vending machine
Dating from the late 1930s, this American counter-top perfume dispenser was first installed in the Hilton Hotel in Las Vegas. Offering a variety of scents, including Schiaparelli's "Shocking", it still contains its tube-shaped miniatures.

1980s & 1990s

The late 20thC has seen the creation of many interesting flacons, reflecting contemporary life-styles and ideals. The "power" fragrances of the 1980s were targeted at a new generation of shoulder-padded executives. Big sellers included "Giorgio, Beverly Hills" (c.1981), whose manufacturers pioneered the use of scented strips in magazines, and Christian Dior's "Poison" (1985), a name that summed up the hard-edged feel of the period. The 1990s saw a change in trends: environmental issues became a matter of general concern, aromatherapy enjoyed a resurgence, and a more natural look came to the fore. Designer scents capturing this new mood included Thierry Mugler's "Angel" (1994), its bottle made from recycled glass, and Issey Miyake's "Eau d'Issey" (1994), inspired by the "smell" of water, and housed in a conical flask that became an icon of late 20thC design.

◄ **Celebrity perfumes**
In recent times, celebrities ranging from the actress Cher to the opera singer Luciano Pavarotti have all launched fragrances, some with more success than others. "Passion", the first perfume to carry the name of the actress Elizabeth Taylor, appeared in 1987, and was followed in the 1990s by her "Fragrant Jewels" collection. This miniature diamanté-studded flask was created for "White Diamonds". Taylor's bottles are already becoming collectors' items.

► **Modern art**
This bottle was designed by the French sculptress Niki de Saint-Phalle. She became well known in the 1960s for her assemblages, which included bags of paint that she shot open with a pistol. A retrospective of Saint-Phalle's work was held at the Pompidou Center in Paris in 1980, and this bottle was created in the same decade. The top is decorated with two intertwined serpents, traditional emblems of love and passion. The owner of the example shown above bought it as a collector's piece and has left it unopened in order to preserve its value.

"White Diamonds" by Elizabeth Taylor, miniature flacon with pouch, 1990s, $16–25

"First edition", bottle by Niki de Saint-Phalle, 1980s, $82–99

▼Surrealist revival

In the 1940s and 1950s the artist Salvador Dalí (1904–90) created flacons for Schiaparelli and Marquay (see pp.47 and 50). In 1981 Dalí was invited by the fragrance company Cofci to create a new perfume line, and Parfums Salvador Dalí was launched in 1985. The box and bottle for "Laguna" are shown below. The Surrealist nose-and-lips design was taken from a painting by Dalí of the goddess Aphrodite. Dalí is said to have chosen the notes of the perfume himself: rose in celebration of his wife Gala's rose garden, and jasmine because he liked to wear a sprig behind his ear and believed the plant to be a hallucinogen. However, the main attraction of this scent for collectors lies not in its fragrance but in the Dalí name and presentation.

"Laguna" by Salvador Dalí, miniature size, 1990s, **$16–25**

"Angel" by Thierry Mugler, *factice* bottle, ht 30cm (11¾in), 1990s, **$247–330**

▲New materials

In 1994 the fashion designer Thierry Mugler launched the perfume "Angel", and its unusual, star-shaped flacon has been cited as one of the most original bottle designs of the 1990s. The bottle was made from lead-free, recycled glass and marketed as being ecologically sound. The perfume itself is an unusual blend, containing chocolate, honey, and cinnamon, translating the contemporary fascination with cuisine into a different medium. The bottle shown above is a *factice* (a large shop-window dummy).

Modern collectibles

Many fragrance companies now produce limited-edition flasks for the collectors' market. When buying modern perfumes, look for the unusual, such as Christmas gift sets or items produced for a special promotion, and remember to preserve all the associated ephemera. Perfumes that are quickly withdrawn from the marketplace can also have rarity value.

▼Pop style

The curvaceous bottle seen below (left) is a modern version by Jean Paul Gaultier of the 1930s bottle created for Schiaparelli's "Shocking" (see p.46), modeled on Mae West. Gaultier's bottle is said to have been inspired by Madonna. The bottle on the right is effectively a self-portrait and sports the French *matelot* ("sailor") sweater that has become Gaultier's trademark.

Left to right: *factice* bottles by Jean Paul Gaultier, ht 30cm (11¾in), 1990s, **$412–528** each

Where to buy

Major auction houses hold occasional specialist sales, and will often include perfume bottles as part of other auctions (e.g. Victorian glass and Art Deco sales). Bottles will often be found in general antiques shops, and car trunk sales and flea markets can be a good source for bargains, particularly for more recent commercial bottles. When buying from a dealer, always ask for a receipt giving a full description of a bottle and its price. This is useful for insurance and is the first step in cataloguing a collection. A specialist club can put you in contact with dealers and collectors and is a good source for advice and information. Like many dealers and perfume manufacturers, they are increasingly using Web sites, and it is worth surfing the Internet for news and contacts.

COLLECTORS' CLUBS &
SOCIETIES
United Kingdom
UK Perfume Bottle
Collectors' Club
5/8 Saville Row
Bath BA1 2QP
tel: 01225 448488

United States
International Perfume
Bottle Association
3314 Shamrock Road
Tampa, FL 33629
tel: 813 837 5845

Mini-scents Club
Apt. 21, 1123 N Flores St
West Hollywood, CA 90069
tel: 213 654 0277
fax: 213 656 7477

Europe
Flacon Collectors Club
PO Box 950149
8157 Munich, Germany
Associazione Italiana
Collezionisti Bottiglie Mignon
Via Asiago 16
60124 Ancona
Italy

Bottle Talk
Estherdal 14
5551 BL
Valkenswaard
The Netherlands

DEALERS
United Kingdom
Louise Ayre
Alfie's Antique Market
13–25 Church Street
London NW8 8DT
tel: 0181 467 7360

Vanessa Billings
Admiral Vernon Arcade
Portobello Road
London W11
tel: 0181 665 9578

Dorrie Buckley
Admiral Vernon Arcade
Portobello Road
London W11
tel: 0973 229 039

Nicky Gould
Harris Arcade
161 Portobello Road
London W11
tel: 0171 727 6788

Andrew Lineham Fine Glass
The Mall Antiques Arcade
Camden Passage
London N1 0PD
tel: 0171 704 0195
fax: 01243 576241

Susan Turner
Le Boudoir
Bartlett Street Antique Centre
Bartlett Street
Bath BA1 2QZ
tel/fax: 0117 960 8309

June Victor
Alfie's Antique Market
13–25 Church Street
London NW8 8DT
tel: 0181 789 5856

United States
Madeleine Frane's
Past Pleasures
Antique Center of Dania
3 North Federal Highway
Dania, FL 33004
tel: 954 584 0009
fax: 954 584 0014

Stephen Kraynak
P.O. Box 82093
Columbus, OH 43202

Ken Leach
Gallery # 47
1050 2nd Avenue
New York, NY 10022
tel: 800 942 0550
fax: 212 352 4403

Europe
Betty de Stefano
Collectors Gallery
17 rue Lebeau
1000 Brussels
Belgium
tel/fax: 32 2 644 2752

Frédéric Marchand
6 rue Montfauchon
75006 Paris
France
tel: 33 1 4354 32 82

George Stam
Perfume Presentations,
1900–1959
P.O. Box 506
CH-1814 La Tour-de-Peilz
Switzerland
tel: 41 21 97721 24
fax: 41 21 97721 20

MUSEUMS & GALLERIES

Victoria & Albert Museum
(general collection of
decorative arts)
South Kensington
London SW7 2RL
tel: 0171 938 8500

Harris Museum
(19thC and 20thC
perfume bottles)
The Market Square
Preston, Lancashire PR1 2PP
tel: 01772 258 248

The Ruth Warner Collection
(20thC commercial perfume
bottles) by appointment only
tel: 01233 636 185

Wellcome Collection of the
History of Medicine
(pomanders)
Science Museum
South Kensington
London SW7 2DD
tel: 0171 938 8000

What to read

Angeloglou, M. A History of
Make-up (London, 1992)

Atlas, M. and Monniot, A.
Un Siècle d'Echantillons Guerlain
(Toulouse, 1995)

**Compagnie des Cristalleries
de Baccarat** Baccarat, The
Perfume Bottles (Paris, 1986)

Barille, E. Coty (Paris, 1995)

Barille, E. and Laroze, C.
The Book of Perfume
(Paris and New York, 1995)

Ball, J. D. and Torem, D. H.
Commercial Fragrance Bottles
(West Chester, 1993)

Brine, L. and Whitaker, N.
Scent Bottles Through the Ages:
An A-Z Pictorial (Bath, 1998)

Foster, Kate Scent Bottles
(London, 1966)

Irvine, S. Perfume
(London, 1995)

Jones-North, J. Commercial
Perfume Bottles
(West Chester, 1987)

Jones-North, J.
Czechoslovakian Perfume Bottles
and Boudoir Accessories
(Marietta, 1990)

Kennett, F. History of Perfume
(London, 1975)

Launert, E. Perfume and
Pomanders (Munich, 1987)

Leach, K. Perfume
Presentation: 100 Years of
Artistry (New York, 1997)

Lefkowith, C. M. The Art
of Perfume (London, 1994)
Mini Flacons International
(Wiesbaden, 1996)

Pavia, F. The World of Perfume
(Paris, 1995)

Rimmel, E. The Book of
Perfumes (London, 1867)

Schiaparelli, E. Shocking Life
(London, 1954)

Thompson, C. J. S. The
Mystery and Lure of Perfume
(London, 1927)

Trueman, J. The Romantic
Story of Scent (Vienna, 1975)

Walker, A. Scent Bottles
(Princes Risborough, 1994)

Index

Acknowledgments

The publishers would like to thank the following dealers, collectors, and auction houses for supplying pictures for use in this book or for allowing their pieces to be photographed. Special thanks to Grays Antique Market, 1–7 Davies Mews, London, W1.

Jacket photograph OPG/SC

1 OPG; **2** OPG/SC; **5** OPG/TR/Be; **6t** P, **b** OPG/TR/AA; **7** OPG/TR/Be; **9t** OPG/TR/Br, **b** OPG/TR/Hux; **10–11** all OPG/TR/PA; **12t** OPG/TR/Br, **b** OPG/TR/Br; **13t** OPG/TR/Br, **c** OPG/TR/Br, **b** OPG; **14l** LB, **r** OPG/TR/AA; **15tl** OPG/TR/AA, **tr** OPG/TR/SS, **b** OPG/TR/Br; **16l** OPG/TR/Br, **r** OPG/TR/AA; **17l** OPG/TR/Br, **r** OPG/TR/Br, **c** OPG/TR/Br; **18l** OPG/TR/Br, **r** OPG/TR/Br; **19t** OPG/TR/Br, **cl** OPG/TR/Br, **cr** OPG/TR/Br; **20l** OPG/TR/Br, **r** OPG/TR/Br, **21tl** OPG, **tr** OPG/TR/Br, **b** OPG/TR/Br; **22l** OPG/TR/Br, **r** OPG/TR/Br, **c** OPG/TR/SS; **23l** OPG/TR/SS, **r** OPG/TR/Br, **c** OPG/TR/Br; **24r** OPG, **tl** OPG/TR/AA, **bl** OPG/TR/AA; **25l** OPG, **r** OPG, **c** OPG/TR/Br; **26r** OPG/TR/Br, **tl** OPG/TR/Br, **bl** OPG/TR/Br; **27tl** OPG/TR/Br, **tr** OPG/TR/Br, **c** OPG/TR/Br, **b** OPG/TR/AA; **28l** OPG/TR/GF, **r** OPG/TR/Br; **29t** OPG/TR/GF, **bl** P, **br** OPG/TR/GF; **30l** OPG/TR/GF, **tr** OPG/TR/Be, **br** OPG/TR/Be; **31l** OPG/TR/Be, **r** OPG/TR/Be, **c** OPG/TR/Be; **32t** OPG/TR/Be, **b** P; **33l** P, **r** OPG/TR/Be, **c** OPG/TR/Be; **34l** OPG/TR/Be, **r** OPG/TR/GF; **35t** OPG/TR/Be, **bl** OPG/TR/Br, **br** P; **36t** OPG/TR/Be, **b** OPG/TR/Br; **37t** OPG/TR/Br, **bl** OPG/TR/Br, **br** OPG/TR/Be; **38tl** OPG/TR/Be, **tr** OPG/TR/GF, **b** OPG/TR/Br; **39t** OPG/TR/Br, **c** OPG/TR/Hux, **b** OPG/TR/Br; **40l** OPG/TR/Be, **tr** OPG/TR/Be, **br** OPG/TR/Be; **41t** OPG/TR/Be, **c** OPG/TR/Be, **b** OPG/TR/Be; **42r** OPG/TR/Be, **tl** OPG/TR/Be, **bl** OPG/TR/GF; **43t** OPG/TR/Br, **b** OPG/TR/Be; **44l** OPG/TR/Be, **r** OPG/TR/Be; **45r** OPG/TR/Be, **tl** OPG/TR/Be, **bl** OPG/TR/Be; **46l** OPG/TR/Be, **r** OPG/TR/Be; **47tl** OPG/TR/Be, **tr** OPG/TR/Br, **b** OPG/TR/GF; **48l** OPG/TR/Be, **r** OPG/TR/Br; **49tl** OPG/TR/Be, **tr** OPG/TR/Be, **b** OPG/TR/Br; **50l** OPG/TR/Be, **r** OPG/TR/Br, **cl** OPG/TR/Be, **cr** OPG/TR/Be; **51l** OPG/TR/Be, **r** OPG/TR/Br, **c** OPG/TR/Br; **52t** OPG/TR/Tag, **b** OPG/TR/Tag; **53t** OPG/TR/Br, **bl** OPG/TR/Hux, **br** OPG/TR/Hux; **54l** OPG/TR/Br, **tr** OPG/TR/Br, **br** OPG/TR/Br; **55t** OPG/TR/Hux, **c** OPG/TR/Br, **b** OPG/TR/Br; **56l** OPG/TR/Br, **r** OPG/TR/Br; **57tl** OPG/TR/GF, **cl** OPG/TR/GF, **cr** OPG/TR/Br, **bl** OPG/TR/Br; **58l** OPG/TR/Br, **r** OPG/TR/GF; **59t** OPG/TR/Be, **bl** OPG/TR/Br, **br** OPG/TR/Br

Key

t top, **b** bottom, **l** left, **r** right, **c** centre
LB Lynda Brine, UK Perfume Bottle Collectors' Club
P Phillips, London
OPG Octopus Publishing Group Ltd
OPG/SC Octopus Publishing Group Ltd (Stuart Chorley)
OPG/TR Octopus Publishing Group Ltd (Tim Ridley)
AA taken at Arca Antiques, Unit 351, Grays, London
Be taken at Linda Bee, Unit J20–21, Grays, London
Br taken at Lynda Brine, Assembly Antiques Centre, 5–8 Saville Row, Bath, BA1 2QP
GF taken at Garady-Feuchtwanger collection
Hux taken at David Huxtable, Stand S03/05, Alfie's Antique Market, London
PA taken at Pars Antiques, Units A14–15, Grays, London
SS taken at Margaret Soane-Sands, Unit 322, Grays, London
Tag taken at Tagore, Units 302–303, Grays, London